WALKING

A Beginner's Guide

James
Carron

First published in Great Britain in 2010 by
Need2Know
Remus House
Coltsfoot Drive
Peterborough
PE2 9JX
Telephone 01733 898103
Fax 01733 313524
www.need2knowbooks.co.uk

Need2Know is an imprint of Forward Press Ltd.
www.forwardpress.co.uk
All Rights Reserved
© James Carron 2010
SB ISBN 978-1-86144-101-0
Cover photograph: Dreamstime

Contents

Introduction

Walking is without doubt the healthiest way to get around. The majority of us do it in our everyday lives, whether it is to the shops, to work or just to the nearest bus stop. But walking can be so much more than just a means of urban commute or an environmentally-friendly way of getting from A to B. It can make you fitter and more active and take you out into the glorious British countryside for an invigorating dose of fresh air.

Two feet will transport you to places a car or bus will never reach. They will lead you through strikingly beautiful rural scenery, across lofty hilltops peppered with panoramic views or into wild and remote corners of the landscape where nature reigns supreme.

Although walking overall is in decline nationally, recreational walking is on the up and it is Britain's most popular physical activity. A survey published by the Scottish Government in 2000 revealed that of visitors to the countryside north of the border, the majority were lured by the promise of exercise and fresh air. Over 70% travelled to rural areas to walk and, according to the Office of National Statistics, the picture is the same across Britain. So you are in good company.

> 'Walking is man's best medicine.'
> Hippocrates.

Embarking upon any new activity can be daunting, but good preparation and planning really will make all the difference. This book aims to open up the world of leisure walking by providing sound, jargon-free advice, covering everything from the basics right through to guidance on more demanding outdoor pursuits like climbing mountains and trekking long-distance trails. You will find out how just about everyone can enjoy the benefits of regular walking, with information on:

- Getting started.
- Kitting yourself out.
- Finding places to walk.
- Route planning.
- Navigating with a map and compass.

- Access and conservation issues.
- Walking with children, infants or while pregnant.
- Taking a dog into the countryside.
- Learning useful hill skills.
- Staying safe.

There is more to walking than just reading up and learning new skills, so to help you get out there and try it for yourself, the book includes a selection of great British walks – step-by-step route guides offering a taste of what is on offer. They range from easy, low-level lakeside strolls to more challenging upland adventures.

There are also ideas for taking your walking one step further, with mountain ascents for novices, a guide to the country's national trails and long-distance paths and advice on other outdoor pursuits like backpacking and wild camping. And, if you fancy going further a field, the book contains a selection of tempting overseas walking destinations.

'Develop a love for walking and there is no telling where your legs will lead you. There are thousands of miles of footpaths and tracks in Britain, all waiting to be explored.'

Develop a love for walking and there is no telling where your legs will lead you. There are thousands of miles of footpaths and tracks in Britain, all waiting to be explored. There are views to savour around almost every corner, wildlife to spot, historical sites to visit and vast landscapes to immerse body and soul in.

Take one small step today and who knows where you might end up.

Disclaimer

The medical and first aid advice given in this book should be used for general guidance only. You should always consult with a medical practitioner or qualified first aider before administering first aid treatment.

Always consult your GP before changing your exercise regime if you have any medical condition.

Route maps are based on Ordnance Survey Popular Edition (1921-30) and New Popular Edition (1945), material revised from field surveys by the author.

Chapter One

First Steps

Why walk?

Walking is the best form of exercise there is. It's great for your health, cheaper than joining a gym and a fantastic way to explore your surroundings.

Walking is good for the heart and lungs and is an easy way to burn calories, helping you stay in control of your weight or lose unwanted pounds. As a low impact activity, it can be enjoyed without putting undue strain on joints and bones.

There are plenty of other health benefits too. According to the NHS, regular walking:

- Reduces the risk of coronary heart disease, diabetes, stroke, cancer, osteoporosis and arthritis.
- Lowers blood pressure.
- Strengthens the immune system.
- Increases muscle tone.
- Boosts metabolism.
- Raises energy levels.
- Improves mental health.
- Helps combat anxiety and stress.

The NHS recommends that we should all walk at least 10,000 steps a day – approximately five miles – for good general health. Unfortunately, statistics suggest that many of us are some way off achieving this goal. According to the NHS, only a third of people in Britain take enough exercise.

'Walking is the best form of exercise there is. It's great for your health, cheaper than joining a gym and a fantastic way to explore your surroundings.'

Some other good reasons to walk

While walking is good for both physical and mental health, there are other great motivations to step out.

- Going for a walk is free – no membership fees are required!
- Everyone can enjoy a walk, whether young or old.
- Walking doesn't need to feel like exercise.
- Walking is the best way to enjoy the British countryside.
- Walking offers fresh air and the opportunity to experience different surroundings and see different things.
- Walking is good for the environment, particularly when linked to public transport.
- Walking is a great way to escape the stresses and strains of modern day life.

How to get started

The beauty of walking as a form of exercise is that it can easily be fitted into our busy daily routines and can be done at any time, anywhere. You don't need expensive gear or equipment to get started and you don't need to head straight for a national park or upland area.

Normal clothes and a decent pair of shoes or trainers are fine for short, low-level walks and most people have a small backpack or rucksack that can be used to carry food, drink and waterproof clothing.

If you are lucky enough to live in a rural area, chances are there are plenty of walks on your doorstep. If you are in a town or city, you can still find good places to walk close to home, and if you want to go further a field, you should be able to find great countryside within easy reach, whether by car or public transport.

'The beauty of walking as a form of exercise is that it can easily be fitted into our busy daily routines and can be done at any time, anywhere.'

Go it alone or join a group

Some people like to walk alone or with their families, some hit the hills with friends and others prefer to go with a group. It is very much up to you how you prefer to spend your free time in the great outdoors.

Group walking

Groups offer a social element and provide added security should someone fall ill or have an accident while out walking. There is less flexibility as decisions such as where to walk, when to break for lunch and so on tend to be made communally or by a leader. Don't worry too much about keeping pace as groups usually incorporate walkers of all ages and abilities and you will not get left behind.

Most clubs organise an annual programme of walks plus various social events, so they are a good, informal way to get to know like-minded people. Many also arrange transport to and from the start and finish point of a walk – handy if you don't have a car.

'Of all exercises, walking is the best.'
Thomas Jefferson.

Solo walking

Solo walkers tend to be much more self-reliant. Going it alone offers greater flexibility; you can set your own pace, stop when you want or alter your plans at a moment's notice. On the downside, there is no backup immediately to hand if you get into difficulties.

How to find a club

There are a variety of places you can look for rambling or hillwalking club contacts in your local area. There may be a club where you work and if you are at college or university there will almost certainly be one.

Outdoor shops, libraries and tourist information centres are good places to start. Many clubs and groups have their own websites, so try an Internet search too.

The Ramblers Association has 500 local groups in England, Wales and Scotland. Walks are organised for members, but they are usually happy to let non-members join a couple on a try-out basis.

The British Mountaineering Council has a list of over 300 affiliated mountaineering and hillwalking clubs which can be downloaded from its website, while the Mountaineering Council of Scotland has a list of Scottish clubs that can also be viewed online.

The Ulster Federation of Rambling Clubs has contacts for over 30 clubs in Northern Ireland. See help list for contact details.

Take a course

A course is a great way to learn new skills and meet new people. For beginners, a training course offers practical hands on experience, often in the countryside, and with all participants usually having the same level of experience or knowledge, you should not feel intimidated or out of your depth.

Courses can take a variety of forms, from evening classes at a local school or college to a weekend or a week away at an outdoor centre. Don't think of it as going back to school, view it as a weekend break or holiday where you are developing or honing your abilities. There is usually a lively social element, particularly on residential courses.

Who runs courses?

Course providers vary and include local councils, outdoor organisations like the Ramblers Association, Youth Hostel Association, Scottish Youth Hostel Association and private individuals and companies.

Most local councils have outdoor education departments offering classes, courses or taster sessions. Visit your nearest council office or library and they should be able to put you in touch. Alternatively, log on to your council's website and try searching under 'leisure' or 'recreation'.

For information on local evening classes, again ask at a library or make contact with your nearest college or university.

'A vigorous five-mile walk will do more good for an unhappy but otherwise healthy adult than all the medicine and psychology in the world.'

Paul Dudley White, American physician.

There are three national outdoor training centres in Britain that offer a range of courses:

- Glenmore Lodge – Scotland's national outdoor training centre, based in the Cairngorms National Park (see help list).

- Plas y Brenin – Wales' national mountain centre (see help list).

- Tollymore Mountain Centre – Northern Ireland's national centre for mountaineering (see help list).

Ideas for children and young people

For children and teenagers, organisations like the Scouts and Girl Guides have a strong outdoor ethos. The Duke of Edinburgh's Award includes an expedition section where young people aged between 14 and 25 can develop a full range of outdoor skills. The John Muir Award, run by the John Muir Trust and open to all ages, encourages participants to discover, explore, conserve and share wild places.

Walking with disabilities

Having a disability, even limited mobility, doesn't mean you have to miss out on the delights of a country ramble. The following is a list of conditions along with some general advice on how sufferers can benefit from outdoor activity. Levels of disability vary greatly from person to person, so always consult your GP or medical professional before altering your exercise routine.

'Having a disability, even limited mobility, doesn't mean you have to miss out on the delights of a country ramble.'

Asthma

Most people with asthma should be able to take part in walking, provided their condition is under control. Walking can improve overall fitness and help combat asthma by increasing lung capacity and improving circulation. Warm up with 10 minutes of gentle exercise before you set off, always have your reliever inhaler with you and if exercise triggers asthma, use your inhaler immediately before you warm up. Breathe through your nose rather than your mouth to warm the air up as it enters your lungs and avoid areas with increased air pollution, such as paths close to busy roads.

Diabetes

Regular exercise is recommended to control blood sugar levels, and moderate walking is one of the best ways to do this. Take insulin and a supply of snacks with you and pay close attention to your feet to avoid injuries like blisters that can take a long time to heal. For people with Type 2 diabetes, the disease can sometimes be controlled through diet and exercise alone.

Epilepsy

Effectively controlled epilepsy should not affect your ability to enjoy a walk in the country. It is, however, important to consider the terrain over which you plan to walk, especially if you are prone to seizures. Avoid paths that run close to steep drops or cliffs and try to stay away from very steep ascents or descents. If you have a seizure, one of the greatest potential dangers you face is striking your head on rough or rocky ground. Walk with a relative or friend who knows what to do in the event of a seizure and carry an epilepsy ID card.

Impaired hearing or deafness

Deaf and hard of hearing people should be able to enjoy all the same walks as people with good hearing, although particular care should be taken when crossing railway lines or roads where visibility is limited.

Impaired vision or blindness

Uneven path surfaces and unexpected obstacles can be a real problem for people with visual impairment. Unfortunately, these are common in the countryside and very hard to avoid. Walking with a sighted relative or friend is one way around this. There are a small number of walking clubs around the country for visually impaired people and some local societies for the blind have rambling groups. Contact the Royal National Institute for the Blind (RNIB) for more information (see help list).

Mobility issues

For decades, people with limited mobility faced a real lack of provision in the British countryside. The good news is that this is slowly changing and, with new legislation aimed at making the nation's footpath network accessible to all, a growing number of routes are available to people in wheelchairs or who use mobility scooters. There is still a lot of work to do, but with a little research you should be able to find a good variety of options.

Many Forestry Commission paths and tracks have been upgraded to accommodate wheelchairs, while canal towpaths are generally well surfaced. Local parks and country parks also tend to have good surfaced trails.

Disabled Ramblers and its sister organisation in Scotland, Forth & Tay Disabled Ramblers, organise a programme of group walks and events, as well as campaigning for improved access for disabled people.

In Scotland, Paths for All is promoting the development of multi-use path networks, while multi-user routes developed by Sustrans with cyclists in mind have good access and surfaces. Also check out the Fieldfare Trust, which promotes countryside access for disabled people.

Summing Up

Just about everyone can enjoy a country walk. Whatever your age or ability, it is good for both body and soul. You can walk alone or in a group – the choice is yours – and if you feel in need of a confidence boost before you set out, there are plenty of courses available that will teach you some really useful outdoor skills. You don't need expensive kit or specialist equipment to get started – and remember, it is much cheaper than joining a gym!

Chapter Two

Be Prepared

For short, low-level walks, you really don't need any special clothing or equipment. However, if you are serious about walking and plan to embark upon longer routes, it is important to be prepared and go well equipped. This will ensure you enjoy your walking in comfort and are ready for all eventualities.

Footwear

Proper footwear is the most important piece of walking equipment you will buy. A good pair of boots or walking shoes will keep feet dry, warm and comfortable, and will help you avoid blisters which can ruin any walk. If you don't already have a pair, the best advice is to visit a specialist outdoor shop where staff will help kit you out.

There are four types of different walking boot, designed according to the sort of walking you plan to do. They are:

- Low level – suitable for low-level walks on paths and trails.

- Hillwalking/trekking – designed for hillwalking all year round, except when there is snow or ice on the ground.

- Four season – offering higher levels of support, these boots are suitable for walking all year round, including on snow or ice.

- Mountaineering – made from hardwearing leather or plastic, these boots have high levels of support and very stiff soles suitable for alpine or winter climbing.

It is essential that you try boots on before you buy. As all feet differ in terms of length, width and shape, you will probably have to try on several different pairs before you find the ones that are right for you.

'Proper footwear is the most important piece of walking equipment you will buy. A good pair of boots or walking shoes will keep feet dry, warm and comfortable.'

It is important to try boots on over a thick pair of walking socks, rather than the thinner socks you might normally wear. Most shops will have a pair you can borrow if you forget to take your own.

Sizes

As a general guide, boots should be a size larger than the shoes you normally wear. However, as with all clothes and footwear, sizes can vary between different manufacturers and even between different models made by the same manufacturer. This is why it is vital to try them on.

UK and Continental sizes are provided on most boot brands and many models also come in half sizes. As with shoes, different fits are provided for men and women and shops tend to display each separately.

Boots specifically designed for children are also readily available.

Fitting

Once you have picked a selection of possible contenders, sit down, pull on those thick socks and prepare to be fitted. Staff in reputable outdoor shops tend not only to have useful training behind them, but most are keen outdoor sports people with a wealth of experience, so don't be afraid to ask questions.

Pull the boots on, lace them up and stand. How comfortable do they feel? Toes should not touch the front of the boot and the foot should not feel squeezed or pinched at any point along its length. Around and above the ankle, the boot should be snug but not overly tight and there should be support under the arch of the foot.

If it all feels good at this point, take a walk around the sales floor. It may feel a bit clumpy at first, and you will probably be a little self-conscious wandering aimlessly round a shop full of people browsing, but go with it.

If your foot moves about in the boot, this is a bad sign. Too much movement when out walking will result in blisters. Your heel should remain on the sole and the boots should not pinch, especially over the tops of your toes. The boot should feel neither too loose nor too tight. If you have any qualms, talk them over with the sales person who might suggest trying another size or model.

The boots may be comfortable, but there are some tests worth conducting.

- Test 1 – if you plan to do a fair bit of hillwalking, you will spend time going downhill as well as uphill. On any descent, the foot tends to slide forward a bit in the boot, so you need to have sufficient clearance for this. If you don't, it can be very uncomfortable and your toes may get bruised. Unlace the boot fully and push your foot as far forward as you can so that your toes just touch the front. You should be able to push a finger down into the boot behind the heel. If you can, fine. If not, the boot is too short and you should try a larger size.

- Test 2 – next, take off your thick sock and try the boot on again. It will feel much more roomy but you are looking out for any spots that feel too tight. Areas to concentrate on include the ball and arch of the foot and around the small toe. If there are any problems during this test, it suggests the boot design is not suitable for the shape of your foot and rather than a different size you should try a different model.

- Test 3 – finally, ask if the shop has a ramp test. As the name suggests, this is simply a ramp on which you can stand to gauge how the boot feels on an upward slope. Try it both uphill and downhill and check to make sure your foot does not slide about in the boot.

Buying online or by mail order

Boots can be bought online or by mail order. This is not the best way to kit your feet out as there is no opportunity to try them on in advance. If you do go down this road, make sure you read the returns policy as you may need to send them back.

Breaking boots in

Although modern boots, particularly those used for low-level walking, usually feel comfortable when new, it is still a good idea to break them in. This removes stiffness, particularly in the upper part of the boot, and helps mould them to the shape of your feet.

It is an easy process. Wear them around the house for a few hours at a time and then go for a few short walks. This reduces the risk of sore feet or blisters when you embark upon a longer hike.

Boot care

Good boots are made to last. With the proper care, they should give many years of unstinting service. Here are a few tips to help you look after your new boots:

- After a walk, rinse off mud or dirt with tap water.
- Remove stubborn dirt with a sponge, damp cloth or soft brush.
- Dry naturally in a cool, dry place.
- Don't use fires or heaters to dry boots – this can damage the material.
- Store in a cool, dry place.
- Regularly apply suitable waterproofing treatment, following the manufacturer's guidelines.

Socks

Boots are most comfortable when worn with a good pair of walking socks. The best ones have extra padding around the toe and heel areas to cushion the foot.

Walking socks are expensive by comparison to normal socks, but a good pair should last for a long time. Less expensive alternatives can usually be found in the clothing departments of major supermarkets – but while comfortable, they may be less hardwearing in the long term. They remain, however, a good buy.

Many walkers like to wear two pairs of socks – a thin pair next to the skin with a thicker pair over the top. This is a good way to prevent blisters. Make sure the thin pair do not have raised seams as they could irritate your feet and cause real discomfort.

Avoid socks that are too large or too small, heavily worn or holey. Don't wear socks that have been darned as the stitching could rub and lead to blisters.

Finally, before you pull on your boots, make sure your socks are free of any grit or debris that could chafe the feet.

Clothing

Dressing for the great outdoors is best done through the creation of a series of layers of clothing, which can be added to or removed depending on the weather, temperature or level of activity. Wearing a series of thin layers traps more warm air than simply pulling on a thick jumper when you feel cold.

Base layer

The base layer is the item of clothing closest to the skin. This can be a thin t-shirt, vest or thermal underwear top. Avoid natural fabrics like cotton, which trap and hold sweat, and opt instead for a quick-drying synthetic fibre capable of wicking moisture away from the skin. Outdoor shops offer a range of suitable base layers and some are even laced with an anti-bacterial treatment that prevents body odour from developing.

Mid layers

Over the base layer, add one of more layers of clothing to insulate the body and keep you warm. Fleeces are ideal mid layers, but shirts, sweatshirts and jumpers will do the job too. Various types of fleece tops and jackets are available, offering different levels of protection from the elements. You may want to consider investing in a lightweight fleece and then a heavier one to wear over the top when it is particularly cold.

Outer layer

The outer layer is the waterproof one that will protect you from rain, wind and snow. The British climate is so changeable that waterproof clothing is essential and it is worth investing in both a good quality waterproof and windproof jacket and waterproof over-trousers.

'Dressing for the great outdoors is best done through the creation of a series of layers of clothing, which can be added to or removed depending on the weather, temperature or level of activity.'

Step into any outdoor shop and you will be greeted by a baffling array of products in an assortment of styles, a plethora of different fabric options and some very hefty price tags. But you don't need to spend a fortune to stay dry.

Like boots, the type of jacket you need depends on the type of walking you plan to do. If short, low-level hikes appeal most, a cheap, lightweight cagoule will do the job. Go for something that is wind and waterproof, has a hood and some decent sized pockets for maps, gloves, snacks, etc.

If you intend to do longer routes or a lot of walking, consider a jacket made from a breathable fabric. This stops the rain coming in but allows perspiration to escape, making it a lot more comfortable. Different manufacturers use various types of waterproof/breathable fabric. The best-known one is Gore-Tex, but others to look out for include Aqua Dry, Aqua Foil, Triple Point Ceramic and Hydro/dry.

There are other options to consider too, such as storm flaps to stop water getting in through the zip (only really necessary in the heaviest rain), the positioning of drawcords and pockets, adjustable cuffs and ventilation features. Go for taped seams to ensure the jacket is totally waterproof.

When trying on a waterproof jacket, ensure it is not too snug and that it will fit comfortably over base and mid layers. Ideally, the hem should come down over your bottom and the sleeves should be long enough to cover the arms in any position and should not adversely affect movement.

Trousers, shorts and gaiters

Trousers should be lightweight, loose fitting and ideally quick-drying with useful pockets. Casual trousers or tracksuit bottoms are good for low-level routes, but avoid denim jeans – they can restrict movement, chafe and become very uncomfortable if they get wet.

Shorts are excellent for good weather walking, but it is worth packing long trousers too, just in case your route passes through overgrown areas containing brambles, nettles, thistles and the like.

'Step into any outdoor shop and you will be greeted by a baffling array of products in an assortment of styles, a plethora of different fabric options and some very hefty price tags. But you don't need to spend a fortune to stay dry.'

It is also a good idea to carry a pair of waterproof trousers in your rucksack, just in case the weather takes a turn for the worse. These are available in a similar range of waterproof, windproof and breathable fabrics to jackets.

You may also wish to consider buying a pair of gaiters, which are short waterproof leggings that attach to your boots and come up the leg to just below the knee. They protect socks and trousers from water and mud and are ideal for walking across marshy ground or through long grass or vegetation.

Rucksacks

For anything other than a really short walk, a rucksack (or backpack) is the best way to carry your belongings.

Rucksacks come in a range of different sizes tailored to different uses. Sizes are based on capacity and are referred to in terms of litres. For a half-day walk, a 15-20-litre sack is ideal. For a full day out, a 20-30-litre sack offers space for more kit, a packed lunch and snacks.

The most basic form of rucksack offers a single closed compartment and a pair of shoulder straps for carrying it. Over and above this, there are plenty of additional features available, such as additional external or internal pockets, hip straps, padded and adjustable back systems, key clips, ice-axe loops or trekking pole holders.

Try a few different sacks for comfort and fit and decide which features will be of most use. You want a comfortable sack that does not hurt your back, shoulders or hips. Your height, build and weight all have a bearing on fit. Check how much adjustment there is in the back and straps, and make sure there is a good level of padding on the back, shoulder straps and waist belt, if it has one.

Also, when buying, bear in mind what you plan to carry. If, for instance, you want to combine walking with bird watching, you may need extra space for binoculars, reference books, etc. If you are walking with young children, you will probably need to carry their stuff too and you don't want teddy to emerge from the pack squashed! It is better to carry a sack that is not fully loaded than one bursting at the seams.

The following is a list of basic equipment that will find its way into your new rucksack:

- Waterproof jacket.
- Waterproof trousers.
- Spare fleece.
- Hat.
- Gloves.
- Food, snacks and drink.
- Map, compass and whistle.
- Torch.
- Small first aid kit and emergency survival bag.
- Insect repellent.
- Emergency rations.
- Mobile phone.

In summer, a sunhat, sun cream and sunglasses can be added to the list.

Food and drink

'Exercise burns calories and they need to be constantly replenished. The best advice for walkers is to eat small amounts, often.'

Exercise burns calories and they need to be constantly replenished. The best advice for walkers is to eat small amounts, often. Sandwiches, pork pies and sausage rolls are great outdoor food, as are fruit, chocolate, cereal bars, nuts, dried fruit and mint cake. If walking with children, include their favourite snacks and juice and reward effort with treats to keep them motivated.

Constant fluid intake is vital for adults and children. Pack juice or water and drink regularly (not just when you feel thirsty) to avoid dehydration. Take enough liquid to sustain you throughout the walk as it is not always safe to drink from streams.

What else to pack

- Map and compass – the most reliable navigational tools a walker can have.

- Whistle – to attract attention in the event of an accident or emergency.

- Torch – a vital bit of kit if the sun sets before you complete your walk.

- Small first aid kit – to deal with any cuts, scrapes or minor injuries picked up along the way.

- Emergency survival bag – a large orange polythene bag, big enough to shelter a casualty in the event of injury or serious illness.

- Insect repellent.

- Emergency rations – pack extra high-energy food, such as chocolate or cereal bars, just in case you get delayed or run into difficulties.

- Mobile phone – a useful piece of safety equipment, but bear in mind that in remoter parts of the country, there is no guarantee you will pick up a signal. In hilly areas, the best chance of a signal is on high ground. If you have one, take it with you and make sure the battery is fully charged before you set off.

Summing Up

Being well prepared and equipped can make all the difference between thoroughly enjoying a walk and having a rather miserable time. The British weather is often unpredictable and underfoot terrain varies greatly, so a good pair of walking shoes or boots plus warm and waterproof clothing is a must, particularly on longer routes. Visit a reputable outdoor shop and always try before you buy. You don't need to buy the most expensive gear you see, but go for products designed for the type of walking you plan to do. Care for your kit – it will reward you with years of service.

Chapter Three
Route Planning

Where to walk

If you want to walk but don't know where to start, there are plenty of possibilities – some closer to home than you may think.

Parks

Your local park is as good a place to start as any. Paths are usually surfaced, making them ideal for all ages and abilities, including parents with pushchairs and people in wheelchairs. Many parks boast a mix of grass and tree cover, offering plenty of variety and an opportunity to spot birds and wildlife. Explore the existing path network in your local park then try extending your routes using pavements, other paths and quiet streets.

Country parks

Country parks are large areas of open space, usually to be found within urban areas or on the fringes of towns and cities. Path networks offer a good selection of easy, low-level walks, with many on surfaced tracks or well-maintained trails suitable for pushchairs and wheelchairs. A visitor centre or information boards at the entrance should set you off in the right direction.

'My grandmother started walking five miles a day when she was 60. She's 93 today and we don't know where the hell she is.'

Ellen DeGeneres, comedienne.

Nature reserves

Britain boasts hundreds of nature reserves, land protected from development for the benefit of wildlife and plants. The majority are open to the public and access to most is free. Often there will be a visitor centre, car parking and signposted walking trails.

National parks

Promoted as 'Britain's breathing spaces', there are 15 national parks in the UK, 10 in England, three in Wales and two in Scotland. National park status seeks to conserve and enhance the natural beauty, wildlife and cultural heritage of an area while at the same time enabling people to enjoy it. The Peak District was the first national park to be created, back in 1951. In the same year, Wales got its first national park – Snowdonia – while Scotland had to wait until 2002 for its first – Loch Lomond and the Trossachs. Northern Ireland currently has no national parks.

'There is nothing quite like a woodland walk, particularly in the autumn when a golden hue descends upon the trees.'

Woodlands

There is nothing quite like a woodland walk, particularly in the autumn when a golden hue descends upon the trees. At any time of the year, forests offer wonderfully sheltered walks – ideal for days when the weather is not so good.

The Forestry Commission, a government agency that not only harvests timber but also promotes recreational use of its land, manages most of the nation's larger plantations. Within its forests you will find a range of marked trails, all graded according to difficulty, alongside routes for cyclists and mountain-bikers. Many have car parks and visitor centres and the commission publishes an extensive range of free leaflets outlining its trails. Pick them up in forest visitor centres or local tourist information offices.

The Woodland Trust, a leading conservation charity, has 1,000 woodland sites across the UK and all are free to visit. In addition to walking trails, many offer a programme of activities including guided walks.

On a smaller scale, there has been a significant growth over recent years in the number of community woodlands, many of which offer pleasant short walks.

Local path networks

Many towns and villages have their own local path networks, short to medium length routes that radiate out from the community. Ideal for families, some may be circular and others linear, perhaps linking two or more villages, or offering access to a remote site of interest or a great viewpoint. The majority follow good paths or tracks and are well signposted. Often a leaflet giving details is produced locally and some even have their own website.

Canals and rivers

Riverside trails and towpaths are tranquil places to wander – and with 4,000 miles of waterways in Britain, there's no shortage of options. British Waterways care for 2,200 miles of canal and river, and towpath walks have the added benefit of being flat with the majority of sections suitable for bikes, pushchairs and wheelchairs. Even within urban areas, canal and riverside walks are wonderfully quiet, green and scenic places and there is usually plenty of interest along the way, such as heritage sites and wildlife-spotting opportunities. Canal life itself can be fascinating, watching boats pottering along or negotiating locks.

Coast

Britain has over 7,000 miles of coastline and over 1,000 islands, creating ample opportunity for a bracing seaside stroll. Whether on beaches, cliff top trails or seafront promenades, coastal walking is just the ticket if you fancy a healthy dose of sea air. As an island nation, we are never very far from the coast and you will find routes ranging from short leg-stretchers to official long-distance trails that can take days or even weeks to complete. Some people have even walked the entire length of Britain's coastline!

Urban

Don't discount the walking potential of your local town or city. Urban walks are rich in heritage and culture, linking places of interest such as museums, churches, graveyards, historical sites and architectural gems. A well-planned

'Whether on beaches, cliff top trails or seafront promenades, coastal walking is just the ticket if you fancy a healthy dose of sea air.'

route will avoid major roads and follow pavements, paths and quiet back streets. Your local library or tourist information centre should be able to point you in the right direction or you could plan your own using an A-Z map.

The countryside

The greatest resource for walkers is the British countryside, that green and pleasant land where you can immerse yourself in nature at its most glorious. If you are not lucky enough to live in a rural area where the countryside is right on your doorstep, you will have to travel, but it is well worth it. If you don't have access to a car, don't worry as many outdoor areas can be reached by public transport.

Novice walkers may prefer to aim first for signposted trails or follow routes published in one of the many guidebooks available. In time, however, as confidence grows, you will be planning your own days out.

Walking with children

Walking is a great family activity, a chance for parents and kids to enjoy healthy, quality time together. Sometimes, however, children require some convincing, particularly if the lure of TV, computer games or mucking about with their friends is just too powerful.

While adults enjoy the simple pleasures of walking – being out and about, breathing fresh air and taking in the scenery – children don't seem to appreciate these delights to quite the same extent. If you struggle to get your kids out of bed or up off the sofa at the weekend, here are a few simple tips to try:

- Walking should be fun, but the word 'walk' can seem rather dull. Instead, use terms like 'adventure', 'exploration' or 'quest' to fire up their imaginations.

- Make it a real adventure – create lists of things to spot or collect, like pinecones, different leaves, feathers, etc. With a little pre-planning, you can

'The greatest resource for walkers is the British countryside, that green and pleasant land where you can immerse yourself in nature at its most glorious.'

set up your own treasure hunt, writing clues and hiding 'treasure' along the way, perhaps tying the theme into their favourite characters, TV show or computer game.

- Take treats to award effort and have a picnic.

- Buy them their own rucksacks into which they can put their treasure and treats.

- Select an interesting route, one with lots of different things to see and do. Kids love scrambling over sand dunes, exploring caves, climbing trees, poking about in ruins or spotting wildlife, even something as basic as a duck pond (remember to take some bread to feed the ducks!).

- Let them take along a friend or go walking with other families.

- Be prepared to cut walks short if they tire.

- Introduce walking to other areas of their life, such as going too and from school. If you are unable to accompany them and don't want them walking on their own, ask your school about schemes like Safe Routes to School or Walking Buses.

Kitting out kids

Like adults, children should be suitably dressed and equipped for walking. Clothes should be comfortable and warm and it is worth packing a spare sweatshirt or jumper just in case they start to get cold. In our changeable climate, a waterproof jacket is a must, while waterproof trousers will certainly come in handy.

Wellies are fine for short walks, but if you plan to do a lot of walking with your child, you may wish to buy a pair of walking boots.

If they enjoy it and you go out regularly, you will find young walkers well catered for with a fair number of outdoor clothing manufacturers producing ranges for children.

Leave spare clothes and shoes in the car so they can change out of wet or muddy togs at the end of the walk.

'While many children enjoy walking, some will remain stubbornly reluctant or refuse altogether. Don't force them as it may put them off for life.'

While many children enjoy walking, some will remain stubbornly reluctant or refuse altogether. Don't force them as it may put them off for life.

Walking with infants

Having a baby or very young child should not bring a suspension of walking activities for parents. Papooses – marketed these days as baby and child carriers – are widely available for all sizes of infants. Like a rucksack, it is important to find a comfortable fit with good balance and plenty of adjustment.

Select walks with solid terrain underfoot and avoid routes that are steep, slippery or uneven. The last thing you want to do with a child carrier on your back is lose your balance and fall.

As the infant gets older, let them out of the papoose and encourage them to walk short sections.

Take special care to protect infants in carriers from the elements, whether it is cold, rain or strong sunlight.

Buggies and pushchairs

For older infants and toddlers, walking with a pushchair is an option, but the success of this depends on good route planning as most pushchairs will struggle on bumpy or uneven paths. Aim for walks that have surfaced paths or tracks for the majority of the way.

Robust all-terrain buggies are available and these offer much more scope for walking families than standard pushchairs. Usually equipped with three rather than four wheels and fatter tyres, they will cover much rougher and more uneven path surfaces.

Walking while pregnant

Mums-to-be should find walking during a normal pregnancy a great form of exercise, although it is worth tailoring routes to energy levels, particularly during the early stages, and avoiding rugged, rough and slippery terrain where there may be a greater risk of slipping or falling. Good footwear with plenty of support is essential.

Maps and guides

When planning a walk, there are two essential bits of kit to have to hand – a map and a guidebook. Maps allow you to plan and plot your course before you set off, while guidebooks offer inspiration and practical route information.

The Ordnance Survey – often referred to as simply the OS – is Britain's national mapping agency. It produces a wide range of maps, including ones specifically tailored to the needs of outdoor enthusiasts like walkers. They are:

- OS Landranger 1:50,000 series – these foldout maps have a pink cover. They map the whole of the UK and contain a wealth of information, including footpaths and tracks, national trails and rights of way information for England and Wales.

- OS Explorer 1:25,000 series – these foldout maps have an orange cover. Again, they map the whole of the UK but with a much greater level of detail. Information includes footpaths and tracks, national trails, recreational paths, picnic areas, viewpoints and selected places of interest, plus rights of way information for England and Wales.

Other maps

The OS are not the country's only cartographers; Harvey produces excellent maps for walkers. Although they do not cover the whole of the country, they target popular areas like the Lake District in England and the Cairngorms in Scotland. Their range includes the 1:25,000 Superwalker and 1:40,000 Walker maps which are waterproof and packed with detail.

The firm's British Mountain Map series covers key mountain areas throughout the UK, while their National Trail maps outline popular long-distance routes.

Map protection

If you are buying a paper map that is not waterproof, it is worth investing in a plastic map case to protect it from damage by rain or wind.

Mapping software

Traditional paper maps are no longer the only option available. Various relatively inexpensive digital mapping software packages are available, allowing you to view OS maps on your mobile phone or on your computer where you can print out relevant sections.

Guidebooks

Guidebooks are a great way to explore the countryside, providing tried and tested routes for readers to follow alongside practical advice on how to get there, where to stay and the best places to eat and drink.

There are scores of books to choose from, some written by experts in their field, others by well-informed enthusiasts keen to share a love of walking with a wider audience. Every region of the country is covered by at least one guidebook. In popular areas like the Lake District, there is a plethora to choose from.

You will find walking guides on sale at a variety of outlets including bookshops, newsagents, visitor centres and tourist information centres.

Selecting a guidebook

When selecting a guide, flick through the pages and see what it offers:

- Are there good, clear maps? They make it much easier to follow a route.
- Are descriptions plain and simple, not complex or confusing?
- Do the photographs inspire you to set off immediately?

- Is there plenty of variety in the routes, in terms of length, grade and terrain?
- On a more practical note, is the book a good size – will it fit into your jacket or rucksack pocket?
- Is it robust enough to stand up to the rigours of the great outdoors?
- Finally, make sure you pick a book with routes to match your ability.

How far, how fast?

One of the most important things to consider when planning a route is how long it will take you to cover the distance. This depends on the speed at which you walk. One long-established formula for working this out is called Naismith's Rule. Devised by Scotsman William Naismith, it advocates that a regular walker will cover three miles in an hour. To take account of ups and downs, Naismith recommended adding one minute for every 10 metres of ascent and a further minute for every 20 metres of descent.

It is not an exact way to calculate walking speed as everyone's pace differs and the rule takes no account of underfoot conditions. It should be treated very much as a rule of thumb.

For less experienced walkers, 2.5 miles per hour may be more realistic, with the same additions for ascents and descents.

The Ramblers Association suggest 1.5 miles an hour is an average walking speed for families.

Remember to add in time for rests, photo stops and picnics.

Summing Up

There is no shortage of places to walk in Britain and no limit to the variety of terrain and landscapes that are just waiting for you to explore. Don't overlook a local park or country park as you may find walks there that are every bit as enjoyable and rewarding as destinations further a field. Use maps and guidebooks to plan great routes and remember that walking is not only for sunny summer days – it is an activity that can be enjoyed by the whole family all year round.

Chapter Four

Responsible Walking

The British countryside is a great resource for outdoor activities. But that is only half the story. It also provides a living for a great many people, such as farmers or landowners who run sporting estates. To avoid conflict between walkers and those who work the land, it is important to enjoy the great outdoors responsibly.

For instance, a walker who leaves a gate open could unwittingly allow sheep or cattle to wander out of their field, perhaps on to a busy road. A walker who wanders through a grouse shoot could put their own safety at risk, as could someone who ignores tree-felling warnings on a forest hike.

Consideration must also be given to protecting the natural environment – the plants, animals and birds that live in the countryside.

'In every walk with nature one receives far more than he seeks.'

John Muir.

Access

Arrangements for access to land differ across the UK. In Scotland, there has long been a traditional right to roam, whether on footpaths or across open ground. In England, Wales and Northern Ireland, there are more restrictions, although the situation has in recent years been changing in favour of the walker.

England and Wales

Under the Countryside and Rights of Way Act 2000, people can now walk freely on defined areas of mountain, moor, heath, downland and registered common land in England and Wales without having to stick to paths. These are classed as Open Access land and are signed with brown roundals containing an image of a figure walking over two low humps. Open Access land is shown on maps.

Prior to this piece of legislation being passed, walkers had to stick to recognised public rights of way, bridleways and byways. The changes came into effect in 2005, following decades of campaigning, and opened up 865,000 hectares of land. For details and a searchable database, visit Natural England's website (see help list).

Some areas in England and Wales – land owned by organisations like the National Trust and Forestry Commission – have enjoyed Open Access for many years and continue to do so.

If you are not on Open Access land, you are required to follow defined rights of way – footpaths, bridleways, byways and restricted byways. These four types of route are signed with coloured arrows:

- Yellow for footpaths – for walkers only.
- Blue for bridleways – shared with horse riders and cyclists.
- Red for byways – also open to off-road vehicles.
- Plum for restricted byways – open to walkers, cyclists, horse riders and horse-drawn vehicles.

'There are around 118,000 miles of rights of way in England and Wales, the majority of them (78%) are footpaths for walkers.'

There are around 118,000 miles of rights of way in England and Wales, the majority of them (78%) are footpaths for walkers. In addition to these marked routes, there are 15 National Trails (12 in England and three in Wales) of varying length.

Look out too for Greenways, a developing network of largely off-road, traffic-free routes in and around towns, cities and the countryside. To find out more about Greenways, visit www.sustrans.org.uk and search 'greenways'.

Much of the coastline is open to walkers, although not all. This is expected to improve over the next decade with plans being drawn up to create a trail right around the coast of England.

Scotland

Walkers in Scotland have long enjoyed the right to roam on just about any land, with no requirements to stay on defined paths or rights of way. This position was ratified with the implementation of the Land Reform (Scotland) Act 2003 which gives everyone the right to be on most land provided they act responsibly.

Obviously there are a few common sense exceptions – school grounds, private gardens, land used by the military, fields where crops are growing, etc. To help people enjoy Scotland's outdoors responsibly, the Scottish Oudoor Access Code was drawn up as part of the bill.

The freedom to roam does have some restrictions. Scotland has a good many sporting estates where animals like red deer and birds like grouse are shot, whether for sport or conservation. Deer management takes place at various times of the year, but the most sensitive period is the stag stalking season which runs from 1 July to 20 October. The grouse shooting season runs from 12 August to 10 December. Most of this activity takes place on open hillside and tends to be away from popular walking routes.

A growing number of estates have signed up to the Hillphones scheme, recorded telephone information lines that detail where shooting is taking place on a given day. For information and telephone numbers, visit www.hillphones.info.

Walkers in Scotland may enjoy the freedom to roam, but there are over 300 defined rights of way, many of them ancient byways or drove roads running through the hills and glens. Generally they are not waymarked, but there are usually green signposts at the start and finish. The best source of information on these is a book called *Scottish Hill Tracks*, published by the Scottish Rights of Way and Access Society (see book list).

The country also has a number of official and unofficial long-distance routes.

Northern Ireland

There are very few public rights of way in Northern Ireland and access to the countryside relies heavily on the goodwill of landowners. However, don't let this put you off walking here. Although there is no legal right of access to

'Walkers in Scotland have long enjoyed the right to roam on just about any land, with no requirements to stay on defined paths or rights of way.'

land, the vast majority of rural landowners have traditionally granted access to hill, mountain and general countryside areas. There are also miles of signed footpaths and this network is growing thanks to the efforts of campaign groups.

Most publically-owned land, including areas belonging to Northern Ireland Water and the Forest Service, is accessible, as is land managed by organisations like the National Trust.

Countryside codes

To encourage responsible access to the great outdoors, there are various codes which walkers are advised to follow. They are designed to protect the countryside, those who make their living from the land, plants and wildlife and, of course, walkers themselves.

The Countryside Code (England and Wales)

- Be safe, plan ahead and follow any signs.
- Leave gates and property as you find them.
- Protect plants and animals and take your litter home.
- Keep dogs under close control.
- Consider other people.

© Natural England copyright 2010. Material is reproduced with the permission of Natural England http://www.naturalengland.org.uk/copyright.

Scottish Outdoor Access Code

- Take responsibility for your own actions.
- Respect people's privacy and peace of mind.
- Help land managers and others to work safely and effectively.
- Care for your environment.
- Keep your dog under proper control.

'To encourage responsible access, there are various codes which walkers are advised to follow. They are designed to protect the countryside, those who make their living from the land, plants and wildlife and, of course, walkers themselves.'

- Take extra care if you are organising an event or running a business and ask the landowner's advice.

© Scottish Natural Heritage, www.outdooraccess-scotland.com.

Leave No Trace Ireland

Leave No Trace is an outdoor ethics programme rather than a code, designed to promote and inspire responsible outdoor recreation through education, research and partnerships.

- Plan ahead and prepare.
- Be considerate to others.
- Respect farm animals and wildlife.
- Travel and camp on durable ground.
- Leave what you find.
- Dispose of waste properly.
- Minimise the effects of fire.

© Leave No Trace Ireland, www.leavenotraceireland.org.

Much of what is contained in these codes is common sense, easy-to-follow advice. By following it you will not only avoid conflict yourself, but you will also act as an ambassador for the whole walking community.

Temporary access restrictions

From time to time, you may come up against temporary access restrictions. This could, for example, be a forest track closed due to tree felling, or a path shut because of bad erosion. Usually a diversion will be offered and if this is the case you should follow it. If there is no diversion, you may have to consult your map and work out an alternative or curtail your route.

Walking with dogs

Dogs love walking, probably even more than their owners. However, there are a few things to bear in mind when taking your pet into the great outdoors.

It should be under proper control at all times and, depending on your dog, its temperament and level of obedience, this may mean keeping it on the lead. If your dog needs to stay on the lead, consider buying an extendable one that will give it more freedom.

There are plenty of distractions for dogs in the countryside and, however well trained or well behaved, they may be tempted to dart off after a moving wild animal or bird at any moment.

Dogs and livestock

Dog owners should be particularly wary when crossing land where there is livestock.

- Keep your pet on a short lead or under close control in fields where there are farm animals.
- Never let a dog worry or attack sheep or cattle.

It is important to consider your own safety too. Cows are very protective of their young and there have been incidents when walkers with dogs have been seriously injured or killed by stampeding cattle, panicked by the sight of dogs.

If you do go into a field where there are calves and cattle behave aggressively and move towards you, you should let your dog go and take the shortest, safest route out of the field. Letting go of your dog is best for you and your dog. It will run away too and you can retrieve it once you are safely out of the field.

Dogs, wildlife and other walkers

On open hillsides, moorland, grassland, along the coastline and on the shores of lakes or lochs, dogs should be kept on a short lead or under close control during the bird-nesting season, usually between April and July. Not all birds nest in trees, some do so on the ground and they are particularly vulnerable to dogs.

If your dog is prone to give chase, keep it under close control in areas where there may be wild animals like rabbits, hare, deer and squirrels. On beaches keep an eye out for seals.

Also bear in mind that not everyone loves man's best friend and some people are afraid of dogs, so don't let your dog run at or jump up on another walker. Muddy paw marks on someone else's clothes will win no friends.

Cleaning up after your pet

In public open spaces, like parks, always pick up dog mess in a plastic bag and dispose of it in the nearest dog bin.

In the countryside, there are rarely such bins. Some organisations, like the Forestry Commission and Woodland Trust, advocate the 'stick and flick' principle to keep dog mess off paths. Simply pick up the nearest stick and flick the faeces into the undergrowth where it can break down naturally.

Please don't pick up dog mess in a bag and then leave the bag by the side of the path or hanging from a tree.

Summing Up

Arrangements for access to the countryside differ across the UK and while Scotland offers walkers the most freedom, the situation in England and Wales has been improving through the creation of Open Access land, supplementing the existing network of rights of way and national trails.

Walk responsibly and know the code before you go. Be prepared to alter or curtail your route if there are temporary restrictions imposed upon it. If you have a dog with you, be ready to put it on the leash around livestock and in areas where your pet could disturb wildlife.

Chapter Five

Navigating a Course

A sound knowledge of outdoor navigation is a must for walkers. Thankfully it is not a difficult skill to acquire and, with practice, it will open up a world of walking possibilities.

Navigation can range from something as simple as following a signed path to plotting your own course over open ground. There are two key tools to assist with this – a map and compass.

Maps

Although a map may look quite complicated at first glance, think of it as a picture of the ground, viewed from above. It is like an aerial photograph with the image converted into a series of lines, coloured areas and symbols, all of which can be readily identified using the accompanying key.

Scale

Maps are a very accurate portrayal of the ground and the scale makes it very easy to work out distances. Ordnance Survey Landranger maps are published to a scale of 1:50,000, so 2cm on the map is equivalent to 1km on the ground.

Ordnance Survey Explorer maps, which show the terrain in much greater detail, are at a scale of 1:25,000, so 4cm on the map is equivalent to 1km on the ground.

Some Harvey maps use a scale of 1:40,000 where 2.5cm on the map is equivalent to 1km on the ground.

'A sound knowledge of outdoor navigation is a must for walkers.'

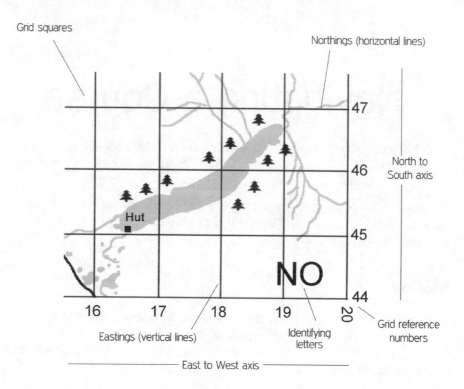

Grid squares

To enable people to pinpoint places on a map, Britain has a National Grid; a lattice of vertical and horizontal lines, all coded with letters and numbers that can be used to create a unique grid reference (often shorted to 'grid ref' or 'GR') for a specific location. On Ordnance Survey maps the lines are blue, while on Harvey maps they are black.

The country is covered by a hundred 100km grid squares, each identified by two letters. Each of these large squares is divided into a series of much smaller 1km squares, identified by numbers.

Eastings and northings

The vertical lines (which originate from the horizontal axis) are called 'eastings', while the horizontal ones (originating from the vertical axis) are called 'northings'. Each line has a number, printed along the top, bottom and sides of the map (these numbers are repeated at intervals across the map sheet for convenience).

The numbers for the 'eastings' are printed along the top and bottom of the sheet, while the numbers for the 'northings' are printed up and down either side of the map.

The grid network not only allows you to create grid references, but it is also very useful for working out distances as the top, bottom and sides of each square all measure 1km on the ground.

Grid references

Grid references are used to pinpoint a spot on the ground on a map. For example, it could be a car park at the start of a walk, a track junction or a building such as a visitor centre.

Grid references can take the form of a four, six- or eight-digit number – the larger the number, the more accurate the reference. Six-figure grid references are the ones most commonly used by walkers and are accurate to within 100 metres.

Many guidebooks use them and they are vital if you get into difficulties while out walking and need to summon assistance.

Creating a grid reference

- Open out an Ordnance Survey 1:50,000 Landranger map and have a ruler to hand.

- Pick a small feature on the map, a single building sitting on open ground perhaps. You will see that the feature sits within a blue grid square. Go to the vertical grid line on the left side of the box (the easting) and follow it either up to the top of the map or down to the bottom to find a two-digit number. This is the first part of the grid reference. Write the number down.

■ Now, follow the horizontal line along the bottom of the chosen grid square to either side edge of the map to get another two-digit number. This is the northing. Write the number down after the first two digits and you have a four-digit grid reference. This number pinpoints the grid square in which the feature is located.

You can more accurately plot the feature by creating a six-figure grid reference, inserting a new third- and sixth-digit into the four-figure number.

■ Return to the same feature and imagine the grid square in which it is located is divided up by 10 vertical lines and 10 horizontal lines, each two centimetres apart. A ruler will help with this. Place it horizontally across the box and measure how far the feature is from the blue vertical grid line on the left. If it is, for instance, 12mm, divide this number by two and you have the third digit of your grid reference. Insert this after the initial two numbers. You should now have a five-digit number.

■ To complete the grid reference, swivel the ruler to a vertical position and measure how far the feature is from the blue horizontal line running along the bottom of the square. Divide the measurement by two again and you have the sixth digit of the grid reference sequence.

■ As the 1km grid squares form part of much larger 100km grid squares, to complete your grid reference you must prefix it with a two letter code, indicating which of the much larger grid squares it sits in. The two letter codes for each of the large grid squares are to be found in the four corners of the map sheet. For example, the complete grid reference for Buttermere in the Lake District is NY 175 170.

Reading a grid reference

To find a grid reference on the map, simply reverse the procedure. Start with the letter code to find the 100km square. Guidebooks quoting grid references will usually simplify this process by quoting the map number on which the location is to be found.

Locate the 1km square using the eastings (first two digits) and then the northings (fourth and fifth digits) and when you have it, measure in using a ruler to find the feature.

Through regular use, the process of giving or locating a grid reference becomes very simple; don't worry if it all appears very complex just now. Practice, as they say, makes perfect.

Contours

A key feature of maps is the brown contour lines. They cover the whole map area and interpret the lie of the land, showing all the ups and downs. Contour lines link places of equal height and show how steep the ground is. Where they are close together, the terrain is steep. When they are further apart, the gradient is gentler.

On Ordnance Survey maps, contours are spaced at 10-metre vertical intervals with a bolder line every 50 metres.

Map symbols

Ordnance Survey Landranger and Explorer maps and Harvey maps are designed with walkers in mind and clearly show tracks, paths and rights of way. Study the accompanying key to see how each one is shown and familiarise yourself with all the various symbols before you go out.

Using a compass

The simplicity of the compass belies its unstinting ability to guide you over featureless terrain or to safety when bad weather descends. It is an uncomplicated and inexpensive bit of kit but could prove to be a lifesaver. By mastering the basics of bearings, it will guide you wherever you want to go, whatever the conditions.

'The simplicity of the compass belies its unstinting ability to guide you over featureless terrain or to safety when bad weather descends.'

The basic features of a compass are:

- The needle – usually red at one end and white at the other. The red end points north. The needle floats in liquid housed within a calibrated dial mounted on a clear plastic base plate.

- Calibrated dial – the dial housing the compass is marked in calibrations of 360 degrees, usually at two-degree intervals.

- Orienting lines – a set of parallel lines below the needle.

- Index line – the point at the top of the compass housing where the bearing is read.

- Base plate – the clear plastic base on which the compass is mounted. Features on the base plate vary from model to model, but all have a direction of travel arrow. Other common features include a scale ruler, magnifier for reading map detail and a Romer scale for working out grid references.

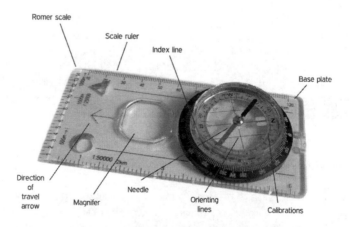

Compasses are very useful when you are walking across open hillside or moorland, away from paths and tracks. If the ground has few distinguishable features, taking a bearing from a landmark you can identify on the map will guide you to where you want to be. They come into their own if you find yourself walking in mist or the visibility is very poor and it is impossible to navigate by sight alone. Whether or not you plan to use a compass, it is vital to have one in your rucksack just in case you do need it.

Taking a bearing

- Select two spots on the map – the one you want to walk from (A) and the one you want to walk to (B). Place the long edge of the compass base plate on a line linking the two, making sure the direction of travel arrow follows the route from A to B, rather than from B to A. Check the terrain of the proposed route, ensuring it is safe to follow a straight line from A to B (avoid, for instance, creating a line that crosses cliffs or a gorge).

- Holding the base firmly in place, twist the compass dial so the orienting lines run parallel with the north-south grid lines (eastings) on the map. Ensure the 'N' for north on the compass dial is pointing in the direction of the top of the map.

- The grid bearing is now on the index line. As grid north differs slightly from magnetic north, you must add four degrees (when walking in the UK) to the reading to set an accurate course.

- Now, hold the compass flat in front of you – don't hold it at arms length, instead hold it just in front of your body, just above your stomach. Now move your body until the red part of the needle lies within the orienting arrow, which sits between the orienting lines and leads on to the direction of travel arrow.

- Follow the direction of travel arrow, ensuring the compass stays flat and the needle remains within the orienting arrow, to your destination.

To practise taking bearings, plan a route using a map and create a bearing for each section. Identify points along the way – landmarks, junctions, etc – and link them with bearings. Write them all down and then follow each one when you go out.

Careful compass work

Compasses are very accurate. However, there are a few things that can knock them off course.

- Keep your compass flat at all times when in use.

- Compass bearings are most accurate over short distances, so rather than take a single bearing for a long stretch of route, break it down into several shorter sections, each with their own bearing.

- Keep metal objects, like watches, away from your compass as they can affect readings.

- Avoid taking a bearing while standing on a metal structure such as a bridge, near an electric fence or under overhead power lines.

- In some places, naturally occurring magnetic rocks can affect the accuracy of a compass. One famous example is the Cuillin Ridge on the Isle of Skye.

- Finally, put your trust in your compass. If you have taken the bearing correctly and follow it faithfully, you will reach your destination.

'Put your trust in your compass. If you have taken the bearing correctly and follow it faithfully, you will reach your destination.'

GPS

GPS – or Global Positioning System to give it its full name – is a hi-tech navigational device that plots a position on Earth using satellites orbiting above us. Many people will be familiar with the technology through satellite navigation systems used in cars. Hand-held devices, working on the same principle and similar in size to a mobile phone, are available for walkers. Although not a replacement for good map and compass skills, a GPS receiver is a handy additional tool.

Technological advances

Over recent years there have been considerable advances in GPS technology for walkers. Early units offered limited features – the ability to plot a position and follow a route using grid references. These days, mapping software can be loaded on to the most up-to-date machines, allowing walkers to view full colour OS maps on screen.

In addition to this, a growing number of mobile phones now feature GPS receivers and can be loaded with mapping software and used in the same way as a GPS handset.

Need2Know

Don't feel the need to rush out and buy a GPS. They are, after all, very expensive bits of kit (GPS receivers with mapping software cost around £250-£300).

GPS – tips for buyers

If you are a lover of gadgets or feel a GPS unit would give you greater confidence, there are some important tips to consider when buying.

- Battery – top of the list is battery life as the last thing you want is for your GPS to run out of juice mid-walk. Battery life and type vary from model to model. Some use replaceable batteries (always carry spares), while others have re-chargeable power packs that you will not be able to boost in the great outdoors (a car charger is a useful accessory). Lithium batteries last much longer than alkaline batteries, particularly in cold weather. Remember to save power wherever possible by limiting use of features like backlighting.

- Screen – the larger the screen, the better, as this will make the mapping much clearer to see and enables more of the map to be displayed. Touch screens should respond quickly but not be over-sensitive.

- Controls – make sure buttons are easy to use and clearly marked so you can quickly access features. Check how easy they are to operate when wearing gloves.

- Waterproofing – many GPS units are waterproof, ideal for use in bad weather. If not, buy a clear, protective cover or case.

- Shock resistance – a GPS unit with a rugged, shockproof shell will survive the rigours of the great outdoors far better than one without. Failing that, padded, protective cases are available. If you plan to use a mobile phone with GPS receiver, take care of it as one drop could shatter the screen, rendering it useless.

- Mobile phones – if you are buying a mobile phone with a GPS receiver, make sure it takes its information from satellites rather than mobile phone masts that offer more limited coverage.

- Insurance – consider insurance cover, particularly for vulnerable mobile phones.

Summing Up

Learning basic navigational skills will really enhance your enjoyment of the great outdoors and prepare you for all eventualities. Being able to use a map and compass or GPS device to find your way over the hills, even in mist or low cloud when it may be impossible to see anything, will foster a greater degree of self-confidence and self-reliance and allow you to tackle more challenging routes and terrain.

'Learning basic navigational skills will really enhance your enjoyment of the great outdoors and prepare you for all eventualities.'

Need2Know

Chapter Six

Hill Skills

Weather

One of the most important things to do before you set out on a walk is to check the weather forecast. Although not always entirely accurate, a forecast will at least give you an idea of the conditions to expect and allow you to prepare for them.

Where do I find weather forecasts?

Aside from the usual places, here are a couple of particularly useful sites for forecasts:

- BBC Weather: www.bbc.co.uk/weather.
- Mountain Weather Information Service: www.mwis.org.uk.

You can quite often find local weather forecasts in tourist information office windows.

What if the forecast is bad?

Don't be afraid to cancel or curtail a trip if the weather forecast is bad, especially if you have kids in tow. At the same time, don't let poor weather stop you going out altogether. If the sky is overcast and threatening rain, try a sheltered forest or woodland walk rather than a hike over open ground. If it is misty, consider shelving the hill climb you were planning and do a low-level walk instead.

'Sunshine is delicious, rain is refreshing, wind braces us up, snow is exhilarating; there is really no such thing as bad weather, only different kinds of good weather.'

John Ruskin.

Watch the weather

Once out, keep a weather eye open as you go. Conditions can change quickly, particularly in the hills and mountains, and if the weather does deteriorate, be prepared to retreat, alter or shorten your route. Remember, you can always go back another day.

Weather can also affect the terrain over which you plan to walk. A lot of rain, for instance, can turn a dry path into a muddy quagmire, or swell a small stream into a raging torrent. High winds can bring trees down over paths, making them impassable, while snow can fall on high ground even in summer.

Trekking poles

When you are out walking, particularly in the hills, you will often see people with trekking poles. Although not an essential bit of kit, many people swear by them, particularly because they alleviate a lot of stress on the knees.

Trekking poles look very like ski poles, except that they can be adjusted to just the right height through a set of telescopic joints. Some walkers use only one, in much the same way as a walking stick, while others prefer a pair, holding one in each hand.

Walking with poles transfers a significant amount of body weight from the legs on to the arms. This not only protects the knees and other lower joints, but also encourages a more upright body posture and can improve balance and stability. Poles are particularly beneficial for people who may suffer from lower joint and back pain.

Buying a set of poles

Trekking poles most commonly come with a screw adjustment system, allowing them to be easily set to the correct height. When not in use, they retract quickly for packing into a rucksack or travel luggage.

Poles have a handle grip at the top, unusually accompanied by a wrist strap. Look for comfortable, anatomically shaped grips that fit your hand and an adjustable strap.

At the other end of the pole, check the tip. Some have a single point, others have a chiselled point and some are rubber tipped. Go for a single or chiselled point.

Above the point, look for a basket; normally a round plastic ring or snowflake shaped feature that stops the pole sinking into soft ground or snow.

More advance poles have an anti-shock system, small shock absorbers built into the shaft.

Setting your poles

To set a pole to the correct length, loosen the screw adjustments, turn it upside down so that the handle is on the ground and grip the pole above the now upturned basket. Your elbow should be bent at 90 degrees. Tighten up the screws and you are ready to go.

Walking with poles

Adopting the style of a cross-country skier is the best way to walk with poles. On flat ground, grip the handles, angle the poles backwards and alternately push them towards the ground, placing and lifting each in turn as you move forward. As you go uphill, you will notice the increased pressure on your shoulders and arms. At the same time, the pressure on your legs should decrease.

When going downhill, place your palms on top of the handles and move the angle of the pole forward so each one goes into the ground ahead of you. In this way, you can transfer some of the weight off your knees and on to the poles. Keep your poles at either side of your body and be careful not to place a pole directly in front of your leg or foot, risking a trip.

When crossing very rough or rocky terrain, like a boulder field, take your hands out of the loops, just in case you fall and need to discard the poles in a hurry. Also, be aware that poles do not grip well on rock.

'Going' in the great outdoors

If you spend half a day or longer in the countryside, chances are you will have to go to the toilet at some point. While you may find public toilets in car parks and at visitor centres, there are few, if any, in the hills. This doesn't mean that you have to hold it in. There are, however, a few simple guidelines to follow when going in the great outdoors.

- Never miss an opportunity to use a proper toilet, even if you don't actually need to go.

- If you need to go, find cover in trees or bushes well away from paths, buildings, rivers, streams and lakes. Urine is less harmful than excrement but it does smells unpleasant if too many people choose the same spot.

- If you need to defecate, do so at least 50 metres from paths, 200 metres from huts and bothies and at least 30 metres from streams.

- If possible, dig a hole at least 15cm (6in.) deep (many walkers and backpackers carry a small trowel for this purpose), then fill the hole back in afterwards. If you can't dig a hole, spread your waste out thinly and cover with soil or leaf mould to help it decompose faster (not a pleasant task, but a necessary one!).

- Use biodegradable toilet paper.

- Tampons and sanitary towels take a long time to decompose, even when buried, and should be bagged up and carried out to the nearest bin.

- Pack antiseptic hand washing gel or cleansing wipes to clean your hands.

'Drinking water from hill and mountain streams in Britain is generally safe, but there are some common sense precautions to take.'

Can I drink the water?

Drinking water from hill and mountain streams in Britain is generally safe, but there are some common sense precautions to take. The cleanest water comes from fast flowing streams on high ground, but you should always check a little way upstream first to make sure there is nothing untoward, like a dead sheep.

Avoid cloudy or muddy-looking streams or rivers and don't take water from streams crossing land where there is livestock, from areas of human activity, like farms or industrial sites, from forests or from still bodies of water like lakes or tarns. If you are unsure, you can treat water to kill potentially dangerous bacteria and viruses. If you are camping in wild country, boil for at least 10 minutes, or treat with water purification tablets available from outdoor shops. Alternatively, buy a water purifier, available in the form of a convenient bottle for walkers.

Spotting animals, plants and birds

The British countryside is full of animals, birds and plants and although many creatures are elusive and difficult to spot, you should see a good variety on any walk. Here are some simple tips to increase your chances of success:

- Buy or borrow a pocket field guide – it will give you a good idea of when and where to see flora and fauna and the tell-tale signs you need to look for. Select one with good photographs or drawings.

- Keep your eyes and ears open – more often than not you will chance upon an animal or bird, so keep your eyes peeled and be ready.

- Go quietly – animals and birds are easily spooked by noise, so the less you make, the more chance you will have of seeing something.

- Pack a pair of binoculars – often you will have to content yourself with watching wildlife at a distance. To study insects or tiny plants, take a magnifying glass or spotting scope.

- Take photos – wildlife photography is notoriously difficult and requires a lot of patience. A zoom lens will help, as will a tripod. Even with a normal camera you might strike lucky, so keep it close at hand and be ready.

- Join a wildlife walk – wildlife walks led by countryside wardens or rangers are a great way to learn from experts. Find details of walks in your area at libraries, tourist information centres or country park ranger centres.

- Conserve wildlife – protect wildlife and plants by leaving the countryside as you find it. Never pick plants or take any wildlife home with you and avoid going near nests or burrows, particularly during the breeding season.

'The British countryside is full of animals, birds and plants and although many creatures are elusive and difficult to spot, you should see a good variety on any walk.'

Summing Up

Hill skills are easy to learn. This chapter has covered some of the basics and these, combined with knowledge of route planning and navigation, should set you in good stead for any walk, whether an easy lowland circuit or a more demanding hill ascent. As an outdoor activity, bright sunny weather is always what we hope for when setting out but even when the sky is grey or overcast, it is possible to enjoy some quality time in the countryside, especially when you can savour views or spot some wildlife.

Chapter Seven

Stay Safe

Walking in Britain is generally a very safe activity and good preparation and planning play a key role in avoiding unnecessary risks. This chapter outlines ways to stay safe in the great outdoors and offers advice on what to do if you run into difficulties.

Know your limits

Always walk within your capabilities and don't take unnecessary risks by tackling overly long, difficult or dangerous routes. This does not mean you should not aim higher, just work up to longer and more difficult routes as experience and confidence grow.

When you are out and about, don't push yourself, or others with you, beyond your limits. Don't hesitate to cut a walk short if you are getting tired, if the weather deteriorates or if the terrain becomes too difficult. It is better to retreat with limbs intact rather than risk an accident.

If you get lost

While the best plan is to always know where you are, all walkers 'temporarily misplace' themselves from time to time. If you do get lost, it is important that you know how to get yourself back on track again. Work things through methodically using your navigational skills – and never panic.

'All walkers "temporarily misplace" themselves from time to time. If you do get lost, it is important that you know how to get yourself back on track again.'

Escape routes

When planning longer walks, always factor in possible 'escape routes' in case you need to cut the walk short. These are short cuts or deviations that will get you safely back to the start.

Walking on roads

Inevitably there are times when you will have to walk on roads. If there is a pavement or grassy verge, keep to this. If there is no pavement or verge and you have to tread tarmac, walk on the right, in single file, facing oncoming traffic and be especially cautious when negotiating sharp bends where oncoming drivers may not be able to see you until they are almost upon you.

Don't assume that seemingly quiet country roads are any safer than busier highways. Traffic may be light but it may also be fast moving.

If you are walking with children, keep them close to you. If you have a dog, put it on the lead.

Level crossings

Take great care when crossing railway lines, particularly at footpath crossings where there are no barriers, warning signals or lights. Stop, look and listen, then look again before you cross. If it is safe, cross quickly, taking care not to trip or slip on the rails. Keep children with you and dogs on the lead. If there are gates at either side of the crossing, remember to close them after you.

Route cards

When you head into the countryside, it is a good idea to leave word of where you are going with a responsible person before you set off, just in case you get into difficulties. If you fail to return at a pre-determined time, the relevant authorities can be alerted and, if necessary, a search or rescue mounted.

If you are heading out from home, leave word with a friend, relative or neighbour. If you are on holiday, you may leave details with someone like a hostel warden, B&B owner or hotel manager.

Make sure you contact them immediately upon your return to let them know you are back safely.

One good way of leaving details of your planned walk is to complete a route card. Some outdoor shops sell these, but you can easily create your own. The following details should be included: your name and contact details; details of everyone in your party; estimated time of departure; the location where you will park your vehicle; vehicle registration number; mobile phone number; start date, time and grid reference; intended route; end date, time and grid reference; emergency contact details.

You can also include information like: what equipment you have with you; details of the level of walking experience of those in your party; the colour of your outdoor clothing.

There is no requirement to fill in or leave a route card when you go out, but novice walkers, particularly those walking alone, may feel more secure in the knowledge that others know where they are.

What to do if someone leaves a route card with you

Note the intended time of return and keep the card safe. If the walker has not returned by the specified time, try to make contact with them by mobile phone. If you cannot make contact, wait for two hours, just in case they have been delayed.

If the walker has still not returned and you still cannot make contact by phone, call the police station nearest the route and they will put you in touch with the local rescue service. They will discuss the matter with you before deciding what action to take.

Ticks, midges and other pests

The countryside is full of insects and while none are deadly, a few bite and others can be very irritating.

Ticks

Ticks are tiny parasites that are common in the countryside. They can attach themselves to wild animals, livestock, pets and humans and feed by biting through the skin and sucking blood. They are most often found in long grass, rough vegetation, bracken and woodland and, although present throughout the year, are most active between May and September.

Once the tick has found a host and attached itself to the skin, it will suck up blood, enlarging the area of body behind its head. Left unchecked, the tick will eventually fall off. However, if you find a tick attached to yourself or your dog, it should be removed without delay.

How do I remove a tick?

The best way to remove a tick is with a tick twister, a little tool that clasps the insect in a V-shaped claw that is then twisted to bring it out. Some outdoor shops, pharmacies and vets sell them or they can be bought online. Visit www.ticktwister.co.uk or www.otom.com for details of available products.

To remove a tick with a pair of tweezers or fingernails:

- Pull upwards slowly and constantly until the tick releases its grip.

- Avoid squeezing or crushing the tick as this may result in mouthparts being left in the skin, which could cause infection.

- Don't use a naked flame or chemicals to remove the tick.

- Once the tick is out, clean the area of the bite with an antiseptic cream.

How do I avoid ticks?

To prevent ticks attaching themselves to you in the first place, avoid walking through long grass and rough vegetation and keep your skin covered by wearing long trousers and long-sleeved tops. If you have been walking through long grass or bracken, or have been camping wild, it is worth doing a thorough tick check at the end of the day, paying particular attention to areas like the legs and ankles, groin, armpits and scalp.

If you take a dog into the countryside regularly, there are various products available to protect it from ticks, so ask your vet. Be sure to check your pet over thoroughly at the end of the walk.

What are the risks from a tick bite?

The vast majority of tick bites in humans simply lead to short-term skin irritation that can be treated with an antihistamine cream. However, a tiny minority of ticks carry bacteria that can cause Lyme disease, a potentially debilitating condition.

Symptoms usually take a few days to several weeks to appear and can range from an expanding and often faint reddish rash around the bite area to flu-like symptoms, mild headaches, tiredness and joint and muscle pain. If you are at all concerned, contact your GP.

The chances of contracting Lyme disease are very small. Even if an infected tick bites you, it will be several hours before it transmits the bacteria into your body, so timely removal is paramount. If you are infected, prompt treatment with antibiotics resolves the vast majority of cases. Again, a GP will be able to give you professional advice.

'The notorious midge may be a tiny insect, but it can have a big impact on walkers.'

Midges

The notorious midge may be a tiny insect, but it can have a big impact on walkers. Common in Scotland and increasingly prevalent in other parts of the UK, including the Lake District and North Wales, midges bite and suck blood from the skin, causing itching and swelling which can last for several days.

They are most active between May and September. Although they cause no lasting health problems, they are a major irritant, descending in dense clouds, particularly around dawn and dusk.

In Scotland, they are especially rampant in Argyll, the West Highlands, the Northwest Highlands and on west coast islands like Skye.

How do I deal with midges?

The best way to deter midges is to use insect repellent. Some are more effective than others. Alternatively, try Avon's Skin So Soft lotion. Although not marketed as an insect repellent, it does prevent them from biting skin on which the cream is applied.

If they become particularly bothersome, cover bare skin with clothing and wear a midge net over your head. Smoke, whether from a fire, cigarette or pipe, also keeps them at bay (although this is not a good reason to take up smoking!).

A midge forecast for Scotland is available online at www.midgeforecast.co.uk.

Wild animals

Native wild animals present no real threat to walkers in Britain and our only venomous snake is the adder, which can be found in England, Wales and Scotland, but not Northern Ireland. Adders have a dark underside and a zigzag pattern along their back. They are not aggressive and will only attack if threatened. An adder's venom poses little danger to a healthy adult, but the bite is very painful and requires urgent medical attention. Walkers are most likely to encounter an adder if they step on one while it is sunbathing, so watch your footing.

Care for your feet

Blisters are one of the most common complaints amongst walkers. Caused by friction, repeated pressure on an area of skin, or extremes in temperature – either hot or cold – they can quickly turn a pleasant hike into an agonising ordeal.

How do I avoid blisters?

Prevention is always better than cure. To avoid blisters, your boots must fit properly and be comfortable. The wrong boot size is the most common cause of blisters. Make sure the inside lining and innersole are not worn. Wear good quality socks that fit properly and remember holes in socks, prominent seams or heavily darned areas can all lead to blisters. If you have bony protrusions or sensitive skin areas on your toes or feet, protect them with additional padding.

If you find you are prone to blisters, pharmacies and outdoor shops sell a range of foot care products, including blister kits with special dressings that provide useful additional padding and cushioning.

Recurring blister problems are usually due to abnormal foot structures or gait patterns. Flat feet, feet with very high arches, bunions and pronation (a rolling out of the feet, so that when you walk you apply excessive force to the inner side of your feet) are all foot problems that can be successfully treated. A visit to a chiropodist will help.

Can blisters lead to health problems?

Blisters can be a particular problem for people with diabetes, poor circulation or decreased feeling in their feet, those with compromised immune systems, and those with other serious diseases. If you fall into any of these categories, see your GP at the first sign of blister formation.

Nail care

Keep toenails trimmed. Long or jagged nails can dig into neighbouring toes, causing considerable discomfort. If you spend a lot of time walking, say on a walking holiday or multi-day hike, check your feet regularly for any sign of rubbing or tenderness.

First aid

Walkers should have a basic knowledge of first aid and carry a small first aid kit. Most of the time it will remain tucked away at the bottom of your rucksack, but it is always better to be safe than sorry.

What should I have in my first aid kit?

You can make a first aid kit with items from the contents of your medicine cabinet at home, or buy one for around £10 from a pharmacy or outdoor shop. It should contain: a dozen waterproof, breathable plasters of various sizes; one medium sterile dressing; two large sterile dressings; a triangular bandage; an eye pad; a crepe bandage; safety pins to secure dressings; a pair of disposable latex gloves; antiseptic cream or wipes; a small pair of scissors.

You may also want to include: any personal medication; pain-killers; antihistamine cream; insect repellent; a pair of tweezers; a cigarette lighter or matches.

If you use your first aid kit, remember to re-stock it before you go back out.

'Walkers should carry a small first aid kit. Most of the time it will remain tucked away at the bottom of your rucksack, but it is always better to be safe than sorry.'

Learning first aid

You can read up on first aid in books, but the best way to learn the basics is to take a course. In England, Wales and Northern Ireland, contact your local branch of St John Ambulance, and in Scotland, the St. Andrew's Ambulance Association. Alternatively, your local GP surgery or pharmacy should be able to point you in the right direction.

Useful emergency equipment to carry

In addition to a first aid kit, there are a couple of other items of gear that can come in really useful in the event of an emergency.

One of the most important is a plastic survival bag. Usually made of orange plastic, they are large enough to accommodate a person and will protect a casualty from wind, rain and cold. It is worth keeping one at the bottom of your rucksack whenever you go out.

Every walker should also carry a whistle for attracting attention in the event of an emergency.

Both cost just a couple of pounds and all good outdoor shops stock them.

Distress signal

If you get into difficulties on high ground or in remote terrain and find you are unable to move or send for help, you will need to have a whistle and know the distress signal. This consists of six blasts of the whistle, followed by a minute's silence, then another six blasts. This is repeated every minute.

If someone who recognises the signal hears you, he or she will respond with three whistle blasts, followed by a minute's silence, then another three blasts to confirm. The signal, which is internationally recognised, can also be given using a torch. Continue giving the signal at regular intervals so rescuers can locate your position.

In the event of an accident or emergency

Thankfully, accidents in the countryside are rare. But if you do find yourself in the unfortunate position where a member of your family or group is seriously injured or falls ill, or if you come across another injured walker, the first thing to do is assess the casualty and carry out what first aid you can.

Protect the casualty

Make the casualty as comfortable as possible and ensure they are protected from the elements. It is vital to keep a casualty sheltered and warm. If you have a plastic survival bag, put them in it.

Get help

Calling out the mountain rescue service is a big decision to make and should not be taken lightly. First, ask yourself if there is any way you can get the casualty to safely yourself. Whether or not the casualty can move, or be moved, will depend on the injury they have sustained and whether or not they are conscious.

If you suspect a spinal injury, you should not attempt to move the casualty. However, if they have a suspected broken arm, dislocated shoulder or twisted ankle, for instance, they may be able to walk to the nearest road with assistance.

Before you go to get help, you will need to note down some vital pieces of information that rescuers need. Mountain Rescue England and Wales recommend the details be given in the form of a 'CHALET' report:

- Casualties – number, names, ages and type of injuries.

- Hazards to the rescuers – for example, strong winds, avalanche, rock fall, etc.

- Access – the name of mountain or hill area and description of the terrain. It may be useful to describe the approach, and information on weather conditions is useful.

- Location of the incident – a grid reference and a description is ideal. Don't forget to give the map sheet number and say if the grid reference is from a GPS device.

- Equipment at the scene – for example, torches, mobile phones, group shelters, medical personnel.

- Type of incident – be prepared to give a brief description of the time and apparent cause of the incident.

Write all the information down as this will help when relaying it over the phone.

How will I get help?

The next thing to consider is how you are going to get help. If you have a mobile phone and a signal, dial 999 or 112 and ask for the police. Once connected, explain the situation and give the CHALET report clearly and concisely.

If you have a mobile phone and there is no signal, try climbing to the nearest high point where you may find reception. If others in the group have mobiles, try them too.

If you fail to find mobile phone reception, do not give up hope. If you are in a group of four people or more, send two people (with the CHALET report) off in search of help, remembering that someone must stay with the casualty at all times. If there are fewer than four people in the party, make yourself as comfortable as possible and try signalling for help with a whistle or torch. Give the distress signal repeatedly.

Mark the casualty site

Make the casualty site as prominent as possible so rescuers can see it. If the casualty is in an orange survival bag, this is a good visual aid for approaching rescuers. If you can light a small fire, this will also help.

Continue giving the distress signal with a whistle and torch, even when the rescue team approaches. This will help zero them in to your position.

Summing Up

Walking is a very safe activity, but like all sports there are some risks. Good planning and preparation, recognising your own capabilities and limits and letting other people know where you are going all help minimise these. But we are all human – however careful we are, accidents can happen or illness can befall us. Learning basic first aid and knowing what to do in an emergency are useful skills, not just when out walking but in everyday life. If the worst does happen, it is reassuring to know that even in the most remote places there are people out there who can help you.

Chapter Eight

Great Walks in Great Britain

Reading about walking is all well and good, but the only way to really enjoy a country walk is to go out and do one. This chapter contains a small selection of great walks across Britain for you to try.

In addition to a step-by-step guide to the walk itself, each guide includes a fact file outlining the following information to help you plan your day out:

- Distance – in miles and kilometres.

- Time – an estimation of how long the route will take to complete, including rests but excluding longer picnic breaks.

- Grade – see overleaf for details of the three grades of difficulty used.

- Start/finish – the start and finish point, with a grid reference.

- Map – the Ordnance Survey Explorer map covering the route.

- Visitor information – contact details for a local visitor centre or tourist information centre.

'I only went out for a walk and finally concluded to stay out till sundown, for going out, I found, was really going in.'

John Muir.

Gradings

The following grades of difficulty are used for each walk to give you an idea of what to expect.

- Easy – these are short, low-level walks suitable for families with younger children. They follow good tracks and paths and are mainly flat with few if any sections of ascent. They will take up to half a day to complete and although there is no need to pack lunch, you should take some snacks to keep you going and something to drink. Comfortable footwear is recommended and it is also a good idea to take warm and waterproof clothing just in case the weather deteriorates.

- Moderate – these are longer walks suitable for families with older children where a reasonable level of fitness is required. There will be some sections of ascent and descent and the routes cover both low and higher ground, or lead through remoter terrain that may be more exposed to the weather and offer fewer opportunities for shelter. Walking shoes or boots are recommended and you should also pack warm and waterproof clothing. As the routes tend to be longer, take a packed lunch, drinks and snacks.

- Challenging – these are tougher, longer walks with steeper ascents and descents. Although there are tracks and paths, they include sections where careful route finding may be required. These walks cover higher ground, more remote or rougher terrain, where a good level of fitness is required. They may also include terrain that is more exposed to the weather. Walking shoes or boots and warm and waterproof clothing are recommended. You should take a packed lunch, plus high energy snacks like cereal bars and chocolate.

Need2Know

Map key

• • •	Walk route	🏠	House
▬▬	Road	🏘	Town/village
▬	Railway	✝	Church
〰	River/stream	🍽	Pub/restaurant/café
⬭	Lake/loch/lough	⚑	Golf course
〰	Beach	☎	Telephone box
Ⓟ	Car park	▲	Hill summit
ⓘ	Visitor/information centre	👁	Viewpoint
🚉	Railway station	🌲	Woodland/forestry
🚌	Bus stop	⚒	Mine (disused)
⛺	Campsite	●	Point of interest

England

Burford and the Windrush Valley, Cotswolds

The oldest of Oxfordshire's medieval towns, picturesque Burford is the gateway to the Cotswolds.

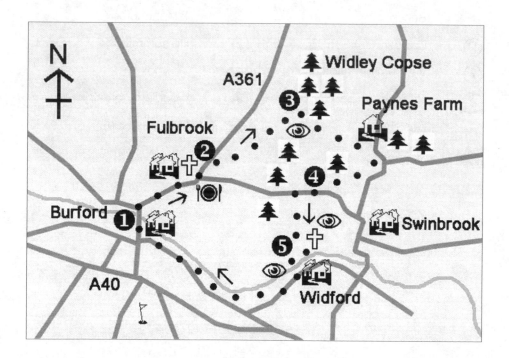

Route

1. Follow High Street north over the River Windrush and at a mini-roundabout, go right towards Fulbrook. Continue to the Masons Arms and then bear right on the path that starts by the pub sign.

2. Steps lead up to the edge of a field where the route curves right. Follow the boundary line to a waymarker and bear left, crossing the fields and head for Widley Copse.

3. Join a track, go right and follow it through the trees. Pass the cottages and continue down to Paynes Farm. Just after the farm, turn right on a path that skirts woodland and descends to meet a road.

4. Turn right and follow the road into a dip where a stone stile on the left and a sign for Widford mark the start of a grassy path that heads through Dean Bottom. Cross another stile at the bottom and turn right at a T-junction to reach St Oswald's Church.

5. Follow a grassy track west past a small lake to meet a road. Turn left, cross the River Windrush, and at the next junction go right. After a brief spell of road walking, a stile on the right signals the start of a path leading back to Burford.

Walk facts

Distance: 5 miles/8km.

Time: 2-3 hours.

Grade: easy.

Start/finish: High Street, Burford (grid ref SP 252 123).

Map: OS Explorer OL45.

Visitor information: Burford Visitor Information Centre (Tel: 01993 823 558, www.oxfordshirecotswolds.org).

Buttermere, Lake District

This low-level circuit around Buttermere leads through one of the most beautiful valleys in the Lake District.

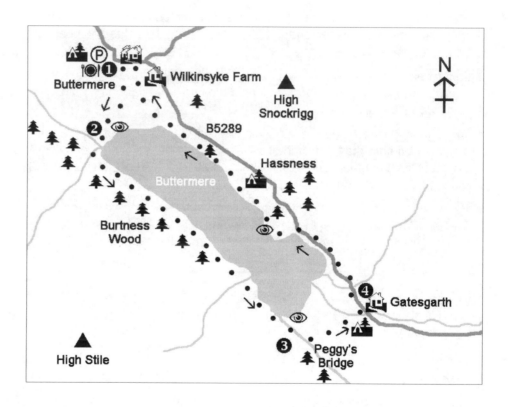

Route

1. Leave the car park, turn right and follow the track through the gates to Buttermere.

2. Head right to cross a footbridge at Buttermere Dubs and beyond the next gate turn left, following a good track through woodland. Continue down the side of the lake.

3. Beyond the end of the water, go left and cross Peggy's Bridge. Cross the valley to Gatesgarth Farm and follow signs to meet the B5289 road.

4. Turn left and follow the road for a short distance until you reach the start of a path on the left, signed for Buttermere via Lakeshore Path. Take this and follow it along the shoreline, passing Crag Wood. The path cuts across a steep crag before passing through a tunnel. From here, it continues alongside Buttermere's rippling waters until it reaches the northwest end of the lake where the route leads to Wilkinsyke Farm and then Bridge Hotel. Turn left to return to the car park.

Walk facts

Distance: 4.5 miles/7.2km.

Time: 2-3 hours.

Grade: easy.

Start/finish: public car park next to Fish Hotel, Buttermere (grid ref NY 173 169).

Map: OS Explorer OL6.

Visitor information: Keswick Tourist Information Centre (Tel: 01768 772645, www.lakedistrict.gov.uk).

New Forest, Hampshire

Explore the New Forest from Fritham and enjoy a well-earned drink at the famous Royal Oak, a tiny thatched pub.

'The sum of the whole is this: walk and be happy; walk and be healthy. The best way to lengthen out our days is to walk steadily and with a purpose.'

Charles Dickens.

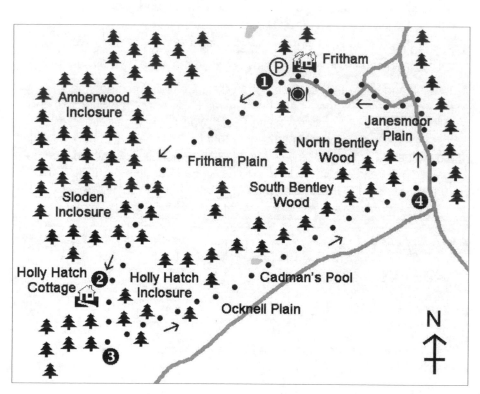

Route

1. Set off from the car park along a gravel track to reach a fork. Carry straight on, ignoring the route on the right, and head over Fritham Plain to Holly Hatch Cottage.

2. Beyond the cottage, the track curves left, leading to the southern edge of Holly Hatch Inclosure. Head into the trees and continue to the other side of the woodland.

3. Go left and walk over the open heath of Ocknell Plain. Carry straight on where another track crosses the route and then fork left to pass Cadman's Pool on the left. A grassy track continues straight on, running parallel to a road on the right until it reaches a gravel track. Carry straight on here, staying parallel with the road until you meet another road.

4. Join the road, turn left and follow it over Janesmoor Plain. Turn left at the next junction and follow the road into Fritham.

Walk facts

Distance: 6 miles/9.5km.

Time: 2-3 hours.

Grade: easy.

Start/finish: Fritham Forest car park, near Fritham (grid ref SU 230 140).

Map: OS Explorer OL22.

Visitor information: Lyndhurst Visitor Information Centre
(Tel: 023 8028 2269, www.thenewforest.co.uk).

Hadrian's Wall, Northumberland

Walking in the footsteps of the Romans, this historic hike links a pair of forts on Hadrian's Wall.

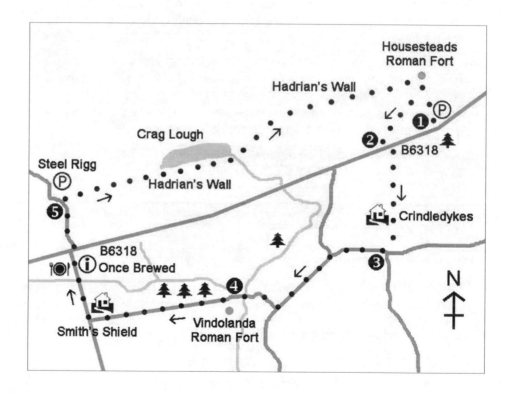

Route

1. From the car park, a broad track leads up to Housesteads Roman Fort and museum, both of which are well worth a visit. Leave the fort and follow a surfaced road southwest, passing a farmhouse and continue down to meet the B6318 road.

2. Turn right and cross with care to a ladder stile. Follow the path signed for Crindledykes. In due course the path meets a road.

3. Turn right and then go left at the next fork in the road. At the next junction, go right to reach Vindolanda Roman Fort.

4. Head west on the straight road, passing Causeway House. Turn right at Smith's Shield and a lane leads to the Once Brewed Visitor Centre. Carefully cross the B6318 road and go up the road signed for Steel Rigg.

5. Before reaching the car park at Steel Rigg, cross a ladder stile on the right to join the Hadrian's Wall Path (signed). This leads east along the course of the wall to Housesteads.

Walk facts

Distance: 7.5 miles/12km.

Time: 4-5 hours.

Grade: moderate.

Start/finish: Housesteads Roman Fort car park (grid ref NY 793 684).

Map: OS Explorer OL43.

Visitor information: Once Brewed Visitor Centre
(Tel: 01434 344396, www.hadrians-wall.org).

The Quantocks, Somerset

Lying at the northern end of the Quantocks, the picturesque village of Kilve boasts a beach with fascinating geological formations and a history of smuggling.

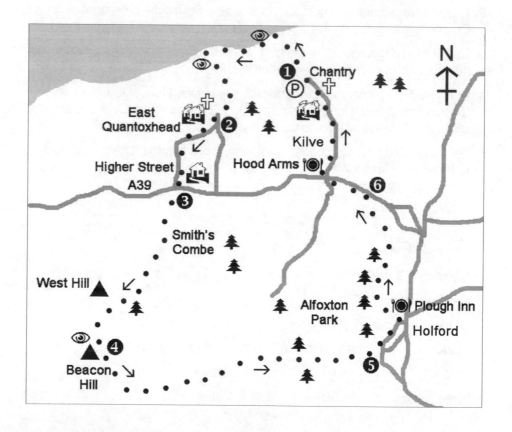

Route

1. Head north towards the beach and turn left on to a coastal path. Follow this along the cliffs and then inland towards East Quantoxhead. At a T-junction, turn right and a lane leads into the centre of the village.

2. Cross Frog Street and follow the road west until you reach a path on the left that leads to Higher Street. Follow the road south through the hamlet to the A39.

3. Cross the A39 and go south into Smith's Combe (follow signs for Beacon Hill). Higher up, the route skirts round the northern edge of woodland from where a steep ascent over open moor leads to the summit of Beacon Hill.

4. Walk southeast from the summit on a track to a junction and turn left, following the track east to Holford. The track meets a road leading into the village.

5. At the first road junction go left and then left again at the next. Follow the road to the Plough Inn and go left up a lane behind the pub. A path (marked with blue arrows) passes through woodland and crosses open ground. It gently curves left to meet Hunts Lane, leading down to the A39.

6. Turn left and follow the road into Kilve. Go right at the Hood Arms and follow Sea Lane back to the car park, passing the ruins of the chantry where barrels of smuggled alcohol were once stored.

Walk facts

Distance: 8 miles/13km.

Time: 4 hours.

Grade: challenging.

Start/finish: Kilve beach car park (grid ref ST 144 443).

Map: OS Explorer 140.

Visitor information: Bridgwater Tourist Information Centre (Tel: 01278 436438, www.visitsomerset.co.uk).

Northern Ireland

Castlewellan Forest Park, County Down

Lying to the north of the Mourne Mountains, Castlewellan Forest Park is a mix of conifer and broadleaf woodlands, sloping up from Castlewellan Lake to the low hills of Slievenaslaat and Slievebeg.

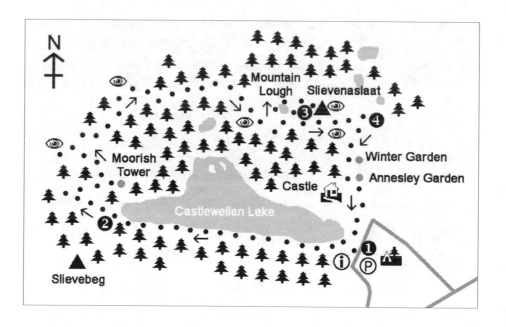

Route

1. The walk begins by following blue arrows along the southern shore of Castlewellan Lake.

2. Beyond the pleasant waterside path, and now following the black arrows, the route enters the trees, zigzagging first to the ruins of Moorish Tower and then to a higher viewpoint. Continue through the trees to Mountain Lough, a small lake.

3. Go left at the track junction for the optional ascent to the summit of Slievenaslaat, the highest point on the route and an excellent viewpoint. Return to the junction by the lake, turn left and begin the descent. The trail heads east to another junction.

4. Go right and walk past Winter and Annesley Gardens towards the castle. A short hike on a red waymarked trail leads back to the car park.

Walk facts

Distance: 5 miles/8km.

Time: 3-4 hours.

Grade: moderate.

Start/finish: Castlewellan Forest Park car park (grid ref J 335 364).

Map: OSNI Sheet 29.

Visitor information: Newcastle Tourist Information Centre
(Tel: 028 4372 2222, www.discovernorthernireland.com).

Glenariff Forest Park, County Antrim

Within Glenariff Forest Park, marked trails lead walkers to spectacular waterfalls and viewpoints.

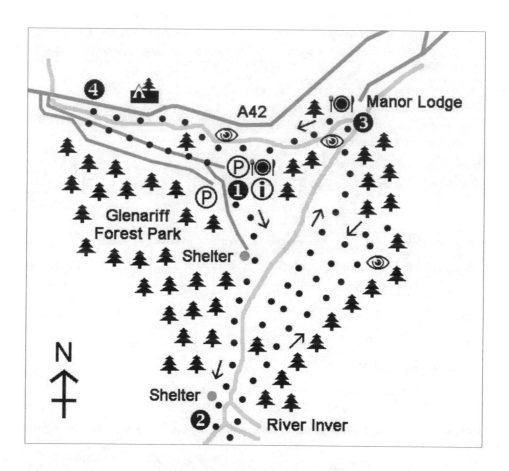

Route

1. From the car park, head up to a café and continue along a path maked with white arrows that crosses a grassy slope below the building. When a track is reached, go right but only for a brief spell for on the left a path heads through gardens, dropping by way of a flight of steps to a shelter. Continue south upstream, passing the first of many watefalls to reach another shelter.

2. At the next junction beyond this second shelter, go left and cross a trio of bridges at the head of the valley to join a path marked with red arrows. The way descends through the trees, passing a series of waterfalls. It zigzags down to a bridge and continues across another bridge next to Manor Lodge.

3. Swing west, following the path up the Glenariff River to one of the most spectacular falls in the park, Ess-na-Larach. Red arrows lead you over a series of wooden staircases and boardwalks into a much narrower gorge. The waterfalls pound through gaps in the rock, bouncing from one frothy pool to the next.

4. A bridge on the left crosses the river and the path meets a forest road leading back to the car park.

'The waterfalls pound through gaps in the rock, bouncing from one frothy pool to the next.'

Walk facts

Distance: 6 miles/10km.

Time: 2-3 hours.

Grade: moderate.

Start/finish: Glenariff Forest Park car park, on the A42 Ballymena to Cushendall Road (grid ref D 210 202).

Map: OSNI sheet 5.

Visitor information: Glenariff Forest Park Visitor Centre (Tel: 028 2955 6000, www.forestserviceni.gov.uk).

Vinegar Hill, County Tyrone

A rugged landscape of high mountains, rolling low hills and peaceful valleys, the Sperrins is one of the most scenic regions of Northern Ireland.

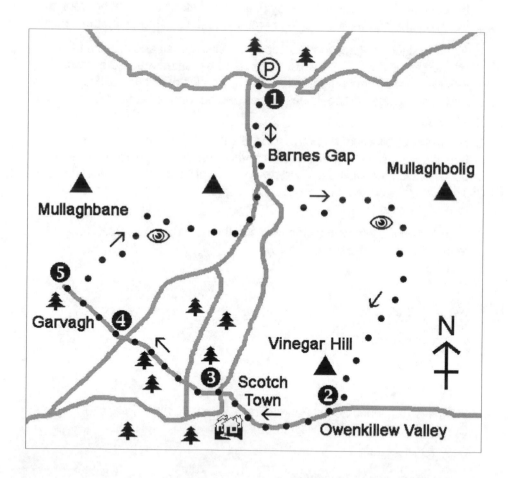

Route

1. From the car park follow a sign for the Craignamaddy Circuit. Cross the road and head uphill, through Barnes Gap. When you reach the top, go left along a gravel track contouring round the slopes of Mullaghbolig. The route climbs gently before descending more steeply into the Owenkillew Valley, passing Vinegar Hill.

2. At the base of the valley, go through a farmyard to meet a road. Turn right and head into Scotch Town.

3. At the crossroads in the centre of the village carry straight on to a second crossroads. Go straight on to reach a third crossroads, 1km further on.

4. Cross and go straight on, walking uphill between farm buildings. Continue straight ahead to reach Garvagh.

5. At a small copse of conifer trees turn right, following a gravel track. This skirts the hillside, descending to a road that drops through Barnes Gap, returning to the car park.

Walk facts

Distance: 7 miles/11.2km.

Time: 3 hours.

Grade: moderate.

Start/finish: Barnes Gap car park, Glenelly Valley (grid ref H 552 905).

Map: OSNI Sheet 13.

Visitor information: Sperrins Tourism
(Tel: 028 8674 7700, www.sperrinstourism.com).

Scotland

Glenmore, Cairngorms National Park

Ryvoan Pass is a great introduction to the Cairngorms National Park. Peppered with Scots pine trees, gently wooded slopes give way to a wilder landscape of rocky hills and untamed moor.

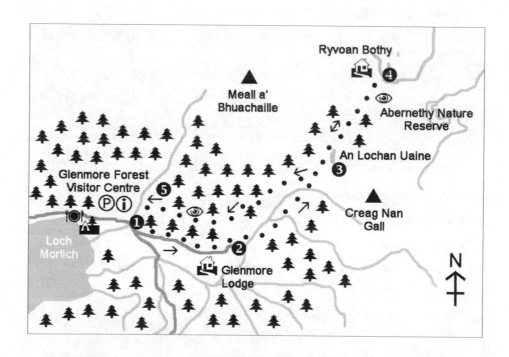

Route

1. Leave the Glenmore Visitor Centre car park by its main entrance and turn left to reach a road junction. Go left and a path runs parallel to the road, passing above Glenmore Lodge.

2. Where the road and path ends, a forest track continues. Look out for flip-up information posts; these highlight points of interest along the way.

3. An Lochan Uaine is a real hidden gem. Lying at the foot of a steep, rocky slope, the water glistens emerald-green. It is an enchanting spot and steps lead down to the water's edge. The trees thin out beyond the lochan as the track heads into open country, entering the RSPB's Abernethy Nature Reserve. At the next junction, go left to reach Ryvoan Bothy, a good place for a sheltered rest or picnic.

4. Retrace steps to An Lochan Uaine and go right on a path that begins opposite the lochan steps. Initially flat, it soon climbs rough stone steps. The path is narrow and the ascent quite strenuous, but it is a great way to explore the forest and breaks in the trees offer unrivalled views of the Cairngorm plateau.

5. Meet a track further on and this leads back to the start.

'Lying at the foot of a steep, rocky slope, the water glistens emerald-green. It is an enchanting spot.'

Walk facts

Distance: 5 miles/8km.

Time: 3 hours.

Grade: easy.

Start/finish: Glenmore Forest Visitor Centre (grid ref NH 976 098).

Map: OS Explorer 403.

Visitor information: Aviemore Tourist Information Centre (Tel: 0845 225 121, www.visitaviemore.co.uk).

Loch Ossian, West Highlands

Loch Ossian is one of Scotland's highest lochs and one of the most inaccessible. The only way in is by train, but the journey is well worth it for the landscape is starkly remote and wildly beautiful.

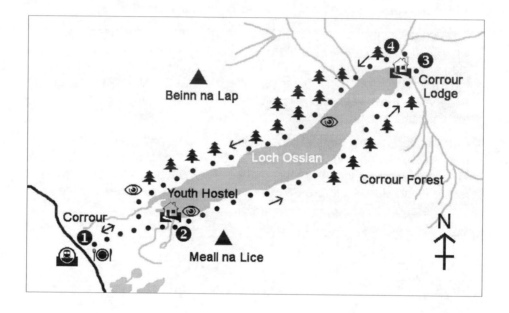

Route

1. From Corrour Station, a track strikes east to Loch Ossian, leading down to Loch Ossian Youth Hostel.

2. Continue along the track running down the south side of the loch. It crosses open ground before skirting between the shoreline and woodland. The track curves round the eastern end of the loch, where estate cottages cluster.

3. Cross the River Ossian and pass Corrour Lodge.

4. At the next junction beyond the lodge, turn left and set off along the north shore of Loch Ossian. Occasional tree-lined promontories jutting into the water are great places to pause and admire the scenery. The track heads through forestry before emerging into recently planted native woodland. It curves round the west end of Loch Ossian to join the main track back to Corrour Station.

Walk facts

Distance: 9 miles/14.25km.

Time: 3-4 hours.

Grade: moderate.

Start/finish: Corrour Station on the West Highland Line (grid ref NN 355 664). The nearest station with road access is Rannoch, one stop down the line.

Map: OS Explorer 385.

Visitor information: Fort William Tourist Information Centre (Tel: 0845 225 121, www.visithighlands.com).

Roslin Glen, Midlothian

Roslin Glen is a mysterious and magical place but most puzzling of all are the myths and legends associated with Rosslyn Chapel.

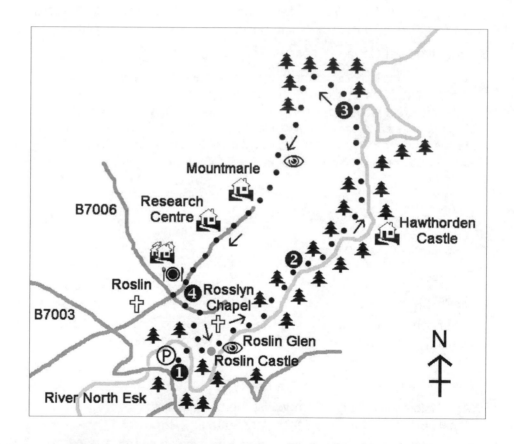

Route

1. From the car park, a path leads to a footbridge over the River North Esk. On the other side it climbs into the trees but just before you reach wooden steps, turn right and pass beneath 15th century Roslin Castle. The way briefly reunites with the river before climbing to an avenue of ancient yews. Descend from here, the path zigzagging down to the river where the way forks.

2. The path on the right offers a short detour to a shingle beach, a fine spot for a picnic, while the walk follows the left branch. After a short climb, the trees thin out and the path skirts between the river and fields to reach a gate.

3. Turn left beyond the gate and climb a path and steps to meet a track. Go left, following a sign for Roslin, and the trail eventually joins a surfaced road leading into the village.

4. Opposite The Original Roslin Inn, turn left into Chapel Lane. This leads down to Rosslyn Chapel. Founded in 1446 by Sir William St Clair, the ornate gothic chapel is famous for its decorative art, intricate stone carvings and links to Freemasonry, the Knights Templar and the Holy Grail. From the chapel, continue down the lane and turn left on a path running between two cemeteries. This leads to Roslin Castle. At the castle entrance, a path on the right descends through the trees, leading back to the car park.

Walk facts

Distance: 4 miles/6.4km.

Time: 2-3 hours.

Grade: moderate.

Start/finish: Roslin Glen Country Park car park (grid ref NT 273 628).

Map: OS Explorer 344.

Visitor information: Edinburgh Tourist Information Centre
(Tel: 0845 22 55 121, www.edinburgh.org).

St Cyrus Nature Reserve, Aberdeenshire

Caught between the North Sea and towering cliffs and crumbling crags, St Cyrus National Nature Reserve boasts exquisite coastal scenery, bracing marine air and a proliferation of birds, insects and wild flowers.

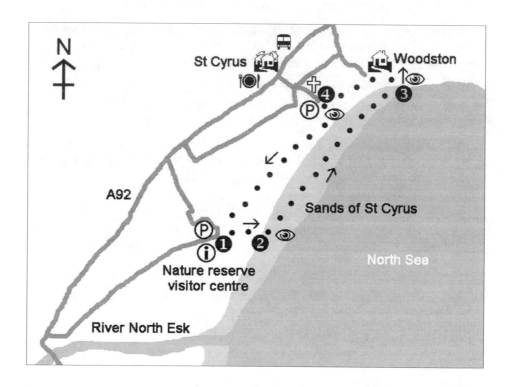

Route

1. From the visitor centre, head across the wooden boardwalks and bridge that span the saltmarsh occupying a natural dip behind the sand dunes. The path rises on to the broad crest of the dunes, presenting the first sight of the beach, the deep blue ocean stretching out to the horizon. Head down on to the sand.

2. Go left. When the tide is low, the Sands of St Cyrus are so wide you can wander at will. Sadly, the glorious sand does not last forever and, as the route approaches the white house on the cliff top at Woodston, it starts to peter out. Dotted across the beach are jagged outcrops of rock, known locally as the hens' teeth.

3. A path climbs first to a viewpoint with a seat, and then to the top of the cliffs where a stone cairn marks the northern boundary of the nature reserve. Bear left at the cairn and head through the courtyard of the former Woodston Fishing Station, now a B&B. A coastal path strikes left, leading to a small car park on the edge of St Cyrus.

4. A path and steps zigzag down to fishermen's cottages in the dunes. Join a sandy track at the bottom and bear right, heading south through grassland below high cliffs. The route continues to a cemetery at Nether Kirkyard from where a more substantial track leads back to the car park.

Walk facts

Distance: 3 miles/5km.

Time: 2-3 hours.

Grade: easy

Start/parking: St Cyrus National Nature Reserve Visitor Centre, Nether Warberton, near St Cyrus (grid ref: NO 742 634).

Map: OS Explorer 382.

Visitor information: St Cyrus National Nature Reserve Visitor Centre (Tel: 01674 830736).

Sandwood Bay, Sutherland

Sandwood Bay is one of Britain's most remote and beautiful beaches. Flanked by grassy dunes and buffeted by the rolling breakers of the Atlantic Ocean, the swath of white sand is a wild and wonderful place.

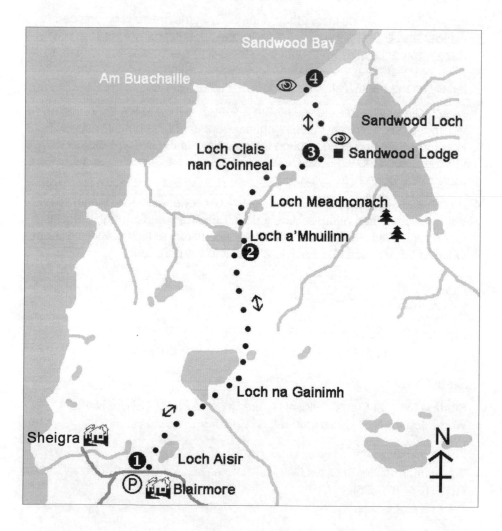

Route

1. Go through a gate opposite the car park and set off along a track crossing grazing land above Loch Aisir. This continues to Loch na Gainimh where the track curves left, heading north to Loch a'Mhuilinn.

2. The track ends and a peaty path continues above Loch Meadhonach and Loch Clais nan Coinneal to the bay.

3. As you begin the descent to the beach, make the short detour to Sandwood Lodge. The ruin enjoys commanding views over the bay and Sandwood Loch. A path drops from here to the beach.

4. Stepping on to the sand, you are immediately confronted by the rugged beauty of the bay. At the southern end, a dagger-like sea stack – Am Buachaille – punctures the skyline, while at the other end, high cliffs – home to puffins and other seabirds – stretch north towards Cape Wrath. Return to Blairmore by the same route.

'Stepping on to the sand, you are immediately confronted by the rugged beauty of the bay.'

Walk facts

Distance: 8 miles/13km.

Time: 4 hours.

Grade: moderate.

Start/finish: Blairmore, on the minor road between Kinlochbervie and Sheigra (grid ref NC 194 601).

Map: OS Explorer 446.

Visitor information: Durness Tourist Information Centre (Tel: 0845 225 121, www.visithighlands.com).

Wales

Llyn Crafnant, Snowdonia

This scenic circuit in the Snowdonia National Park links the stunning twin lakes of Llyn Crafnant and Llyn Geirionydd.

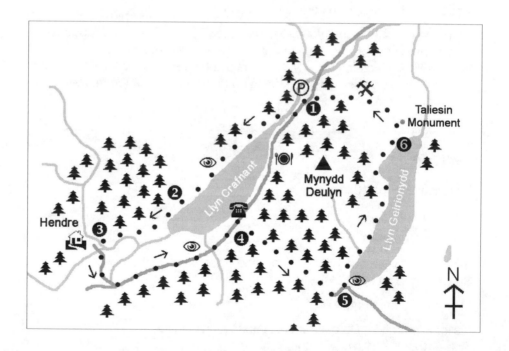

Route

1. Leave the car park, turn right and head southwest along the road to Llyn Crafnant. At the outflow of the lake, turn right to join a forest track that runs along the northwest shore. The pleasant waterside trail leads through woodland and over open ground.

2. Shortly after entering a coniferous plantation, the route forks. Go left and continue until you reach a stile. Don't cross this but continue along the track to pick up a path on the left that descends to a cottage at Hendre.

3. Cross a footbridge and bear left along a track that meets a road beyond chalets. Follow the road back towards the lake until you reach a telephone box.

4. Leave the road, turn right and follow the path signed for Llyn Gcirionydd (there are blue waymarkers on the trail). The route climbs through the forest before descending to reach a stile in the base of the valley.

5. Cross this and head north along the west side of Llyn Geirionydd.

6. At the north end of the lake, go left on a track that leads to Taliesin Monument before descending to a ladder stile on the left. Cross this and a good path runs west to an old mine. Join a track on the right that descends to the car park.

Walk facts

Distance: 5 miles/8km.

Time: 3 hours.

Grade: moderate.

Start/finish: Llyn Crafnant car park, near Trefriw (grid ref SH 756 618).

Map: OS Explorer OL17.

Visitor information: Caernarfon Tourist Information Centre
(Tel: 01286 672232, www.visitsnowdonia.info).

Stackpole Head, South Pembrokeshire

This fascinating ramble through the Stackpole Estate National Nature Reserve combines beach and cliff top paths with more sheltered inland waterside ways and woodland.

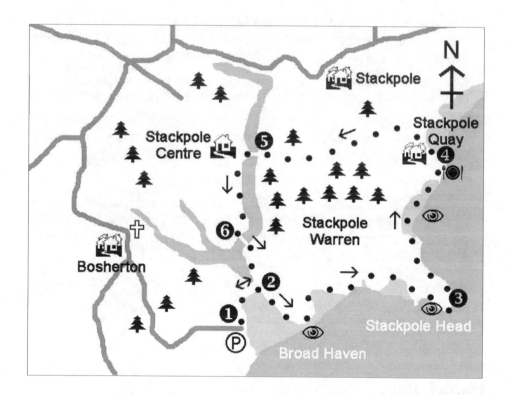

Route

1. From the car park, head initially for the beach, cross the land above the sand and turn left when you reach a stream to find a bridge spanning the water a little way inland.

2. Cross the bridge, turn right and follow the path towards the sea. It curves round the first headland to Saddle Bay and then a little further on Raming Hole. From here, the route heads out to Stackpole Head, home to colonies of guillemot and razorbill.

3. Follow the coastal path round to the glorious sandy beach at Barafundle Bay. Cross the bay and climb the stone steps at the far end. These lead to another section of coastal path heading to Stackpole Quay, an 18th century harbour with a tea room.

4. The route turns inland at this point, a track leading west to a bridge below Stackpole Centre.

5. Cross Eight Arch Bridge, turn left and follow the waterside path down to Grassy Bridge.

6. Cross Grassy Bridge and a path leads to the bridge upstream from Broad Haven beach, crossed earlier in the route.

Walk facts

Distance: 5 miles/8km.

Time: 2-3 hours.

Grade: easy.

Start/finish: National Trust Broad Haven beach car park (grid ref SR 976 938)

Map: OS Explorer OL36.

Visitor information: Stackpole Centre (Tel: 01646 661359, www. nationaltrust.org.uk).

Sugar Loaf Mountain, Brecon Beacons

Sugar Loaf's distinctive conical summit ensures it is a prominent landmark amongst the hills of Abergavenny.

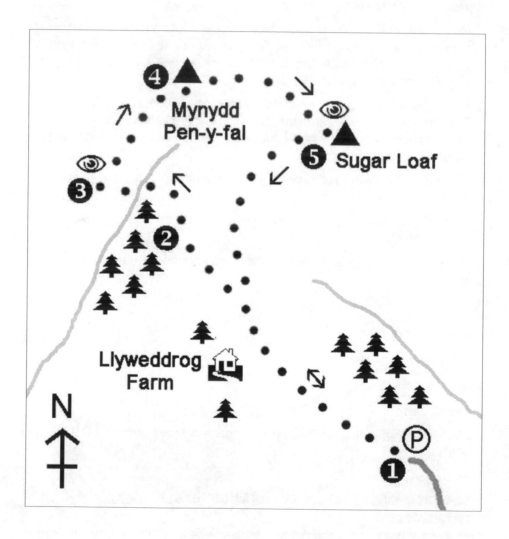

Route

1. Three tracks leave the car park. Take the middle one, a broad grassy route, and follow it to a crossroads by the corner of a wall. Carry straight on here, keeping a wall to your left and in due course start to descend into the valley, aiming for the edge of woodland.

2. Follow the edge of the trees round to cross a stream. The route climbs from the base of the valley, following a fairly steep path up on to the shoulder of a low hill where you will meet a wall.

3. Bear right and follow the wall until the slope finally levels off by a gate in the corner of the wall. Turn right here and follow a grassy path over rough ground to meet a track coming in from the left.

4. Carry straight on to begin the final ascent of Sugar Loaf. There are some rocks to negotiate but the summit trig point is soon reached. Enjoy the cracking views across the Brecon Beacons before embarking upon the descent.

5. Due to its popularity, there are various paths leading from the summit down to the car park. Go west and then southwest from the trig point to find the easiest route. The way drops quite steeply to meet the path you followed out earlier in the day. Follow this back to the start.

Walk facts

Distance: 4.5 miles/7.2km.

Time: 2-3 hours.

Grade: challenging.

Start/finish: Sugar Loaf car park, west of Abergavenny (grid ref SO 268 167).

Map: OS Explorer OL13.

Visitor information: Abergavenny Tourist Information and National Park Centre (Tel: 01873 853254, www.breconbeacons.org).

Summing Up

These routes are designed to offer a taste of walking in Britain. They explore diverse landscapes, cover different types of terrain and offer many different scenic attractions – from tranquil countryside to dramatic gorges, peaceful lakes to spectacular waterfalls. Each is in an area where other walks can be found close by – the visitor information centres will be able to point you in the right direction.

Chapter Nine

A World of Walks

A whole world of walks awaits the adventurous traveller. From easy family strolls through alpine meadows to longer, more challenging mountain treks in far-flung destinations, the possibilities are endless.

So when you are planning your next summer break, why not consider a walking holiday? Here are a few destinations, all of which are sure to inspire dreams of overseas adventure.

Pyrenees National Park (France)

The Pyrenees mountain range stretches along the border between France and Spain. The highest peaks are over 3,000 metres tall, but hidden away in the landscape are plenty of shorter, less demanding trails. The town of Luz-Saint-Sauveur sits on the edge of the Pyrenees National Park and is a great base.

Close at hand is the Cirque de Gavarnie, a vast glacial bowl. Regarded as one of the most stunning natural spectacles in Europe, it is a staggering 1,400 metres from top to bottom, a series of sheer cliffs plunging down from the soaring jagged peaks that rip across the skyline.

The neighbouring Cirque de Troumouse, peppered with mountain tarns, and the Cirque d'Estaube are equally inspiring, if less well known.

'The human spirit needs places where nature has not been rearranged by the hand of man.'

Author Unknown.

The majority of hikes in the region are well signposted. One of the best is the walk up to the Brèche de Roland, a near vertical gap in the rock measuring 100 metres by 60 metres that sits on the border. The route involves a scramble up a waterfall and a hike over a glacier, and nearby there are ice caves at the Grotto Casteret to explore.

For those seeking higher-level routes, marked trails lead into the mountains and guides can be hired in Luz.

'One of the best is the walk up to the Brèche de Roland, a near vertical gap in the rock measuring 100 metres by 60 metres that sits on the border.'

A closer look

When to go: the beginning and end of the summer season offer generally fine weather with more comfortable temperatures for walking. Afternoon thunderstorms are common.

Getting there: fly from the UK to Pau Pyrenees or Tarbes-Lourdes airport. On arrival, a rental car is the best way to get around, although public transport is generally good with bus links from Luz to surrounding towns and villages.

Staying there: Luz and neighbouring towns offer a range of hotel and B&B accommodation. Self-catering is popular and there are a dozen campsites within walking distance of the town centre.

Maps and guides: *Le Guide Rando: Gavarnie-Luz* by Michel Record (Rando Editions) offers 55 walks around Gavarnie and Luz with French text, excellent photos and clear, easy to follow maps. The best maps are the Institut Geographique National 1:25,000 series.

More information: www.parc-pyrenees.com.

Triglav National Park (Slovenia)

A fairytale landscape complete with a pretty lake, an eerie cliff-top castle and enchanting river gorges awaits visitors to Bled. One of Slovenia's most popular holiday hotspots, the bustling little town is unashamedly touristy, but for those seeking a more active break, it is an ideal base for exploring the surrounding countryside.

The Vintgar Gorge is a mile-long ravine where a network of bridges and boardwalks pinned to the 150-metre high vertical rocks creates an enthralling adventure. The nearby Pokljuka Gorge boasts subterranean caverns while the hike through the Mostnica Gorge and Voje Valley leads to the pounding Savica Waterfall.

Around Lake Bohinj, lots of trails radiate into the hills, the most challenging leading up the nation's tallest peak, Triglav. It is a two to three-day expedition for experienced mountaineers.

A closer look

When to go: June to September.

Getting there: there are budget airline flights from London to Ljubljana, 30 miles from Bled. Renting a car is the most convenient way to get around, but there is a rail link between Ljubljana and Bled and local bus services.

Staying there: accommodation – ranging from top class hotels to smaller, more informal guesthouses – is plentiful but advance booking is recommended, particularly in the peak months of July and August.

Maps and guides: pick up a free copy of the leaflet *Hiking in Slovenia* from local tourist offices.

More information: www.slovenia.info.

Corsica National Park (Corsica)

The Mediterranean island of Corsica boasts over 1,500km of walking trails, ranging from easy rambles through lush meadows to more demanding mountain ascents (there are 50 peaks over 2,000 metres high).

For a real challenge, the 110-mile long GR20 high-altitude trail follows the mountain ridges that cut across Corsica from Calenzana, in the north, to Conca, near Porto Vecchio, in the south. It takes two weeks to complete and requires a good head for heights and plenty of climbing experience.

Other shorter multi-day routes criss-cross the island and there are plenty of small hotels and mountain refuges offering shelter and sustenance at the end of a long, hot day in the hills.

The coastal resort of Calvi, in the Balagne region, and Corte, in the Haute Corse region, are both good bases for walkers. Two areas to make a beeline for are Tartagine Forest and Restonica Valley, a stunning glacial landscape of deep gorges cloaked in lush pine forest.

A closer look

When to go: the main walking season is between May and early July and in September (July and August are too hot for comfortable walking).

Getting there: direct flights are available from UK airports to Corsica and you should aim for Calvi or Bastia airports in the north of the island.

Staying there: Corsica is a popular destination for travellers so there is no shortage of accommodation to suit all budgets.

Maps and guides: *Walking in Corsica* by Gillian Price (Cicerone) offers a selection of routes on the island.

More information: www.visit-corsica.com.

Durmitor National Park (Montenegro)

Montenegro is fast developing as a holiday destination and for a small country it has big potential for hiking and mountaineering. Inland from the spectacular coastline, much of the country is mountainous but the area to aim for is the Durmitor National Park.

Bordered by two deep ravines, the park has dozens of high peaks, a network of canyons and a generous smattering of glacial lakes. There are 2,000km of marked footpaths to explore. Various full- and half-day treks begin in the town of Žabljak.

Set aside time for visits to the Lovcen National Park, where marked trails radiate out from Ivanova Korita, and the mountainous Biogradska Gora National Park in central Montenegro. Or try one of two long-distance trails, the 164km long Montenegrin Mountain Hiking Transversal or the 182km Montenegrin Coast Transversal.

A closer look

When to go: snow can lie on high ground from October through to June and the best times for walking are early and late summer.

Getting there: Montenegro Airlines fly from London to capital Podgorica, but a cheaper option is to go with one of the budget carriers to Dubrovnik in Croatia and continue overland from there, either by bus or rental car.

Staying there: Žabljak has a number of inexpensive hotels or you could stay more cheaply in one of the numerous private rooms.

Maps and guides: the 1:25,000 scale Durmitor and Tara Canyon National Park map details 27 marked walking trails and includes some useful tourist information in English.

More information: www.montenegro.travel.

Levada walking (Madeira)

Madeira has a unique network of paths that run parallel with levadas, spidery channels that filter water from high ground to villages and agricultural terraces.

They offer easy-to-follow, well-graded routes through glorious scenery and over rugged terrain. While most are amiable rambling trails, some border very steep drops, and others hug the hillside tightly. The routes are all graded according to difficulty and alternative paths are frequently available to avoid exposed spots.

Funchal is the best base for levada walking and a cable car provides access to two of the most popular ones. One of the best, however, is the 11km Levada do Furado. It runs high above the Ribeiro Frio Valley, offering unrivalled views towards Porta da Cruz, and along its twisting course passes through numerous tunnels (take a torch!).

A closer look

When to go: enjoy walking in Madeira all year round.

Getting there: there are direct chartered and scheduled flights from various UK airports to Funchal.

Staying there: Funchal has an excellent selection of hotels, guesthouses and self-catering apartments.

Maps and guides: the Kompass 1:50,000 Madeira map highlights a selection of walking trails and shows the levadas.

More information: www.madeiraislands.travel.

Slovenský Raj National Park (Slovakia)

Slovenský Raj is a 44,800-acre national park in the eastern part of the country, typically karstic and cherished for its natural woodland, indigenous wildlife and – the reason why most people visit – its spectacularly deep limestone canyons and gorges.

Explorers first ventured up them in the early 20th century, and in the 1950s the mountain rescue service installed metal ladders, chains, steps and wooden walkways, opening them up to walkers.

Suchá Belá is the most popular route. It can get pretty crowded at the height of the season but offers a great introduction to ravine walking Slovak-style. Two of the best routes are to be found west of Suchá Belá and they tend to attract fewer visitors. The Piecky gorge starts at Pila, while Veľký Sokol is the region's deepest ravine with some of the best scrambling. The highlight is Roth's Gorge, near the top. Overwhelmingly claustrophobic, it is a dark underworld of frothy, foaming white water.

> 'Veľký Sokol is the region's deepest ravine. The highlight is Roth's Gorge, near the top. Overwhelmingly claustrophobic, it is a dark underworld of frothy, foaming white water.'

A closer look

When to go: visit between May and October. September is traditionally the driest month.

Getting there: there are budget airline flights from various UK airports to Bratislava and the quickest way to the mountains is to fly from Bratislava to Poprad, but it is not cheap and there's more flexibility in hiring a car.

Staying there: best value accommodation is in private rooms in local houses, but there are some good hotels in the area. Small wooden chalets, known as chatty, can be rented by the night.

Maps and guides: the best guide, with 40 routes and easy-to-follow maps, is *Knapsacked Travel – The Slovak Paradise* (Dajama, 2001). Order the English language version before you go (www.cordee.co.uk) as it is hard to come by in Slovakia.

More information: www.sloevenskyraj.sk.

White Mountains (Crete)

The Greek island of Crete is not particularly well known for its walking country, but there are some magnificent mountains and spectacular trails, particularly in the west.

The classic Samaria Gorge offers a breathtaking 16km ravine walk, starting high inland and finishing on the coast of the Libyan Sea at Agia Roumeli. The route is very popular, so set out early before the tourist coaches arrive.

The gorges of Agia Irini and Aradena, although less spectacular, are a quieter alternative. The latter is arguably more challenging, covering some very rough and ready terrain.

For a cracking coastal walk, try the hike from Sougia to Tripiti via Profiti Elias in southern Crete. Or if you prefer to head for high ground, 1,980-metre high Gingilos is an accessible summit – thanks to an excellent path – with superb views over the Aegean sea.

The E4 Pan-European Footpath crosses the island from west to east taking in the best Crete has to offer in terms of scenery, history, tradition and culture.

'The classic Samaria Gorge offers a breathtaking 16km ravine walk, starting high inland and finishing on the coast of the Libyan Sea.'

A closer look

When to go: the best time for the walker is in the spring when the weather is cooler. July and August are the busiest and most expensive months.

Getting there: there are direct flights from the UK to Crete's main airport at Heraklion.

Staying there: accommodation close to the hills can be found in villages to the south of Haniá, while the city itself has a number of hotels and scores of rooms to rent.

Maps and guides: Greek cartographers Anavasi publish a series of 1:25,000 maps covering the island. *Western Crete Landscapes* by Jonnie Godfrey and Elizabeth Karslake (Sunflower Books) details 30 walks in West Crete.

More information: www.explorecrete.com.

The Inca Trail (Peru)

With the lost city of Machu Picchu at its end, the Inca Trail is a 40km four-day hike through lush forests, over windswept grasslands and across dramatic mountain passes. It is but one of thousands of trails built by the Incas to link their settlements, but thanks to the enigmatic ruins and the many mysteries surrounding the establishment and sudden abandonment of Machu Picchu, this is one of the most popular treks in the world.

Would-be Inca Trail explorers must go with a tour group and there are plenty of trekking companies willing to take you there. With a daily tally of just 10km, it is not a difficult walk, although there are some steep and strenuous ascents, so a good degree of fitness is required.

The shorter Sacred Trail is 14km long and can be hiked over two days, while those who prefer to go it alone and avoid the tourist hotspots may prefer the trek to the ruins of Choquequirau or the walk to Vilcabamba La Vieja, both of which offer an alternative Inca experience without the need to hire a guide or join an organised group.

'Thanks to the enigmatic ruins and the many mysteries surrounding the establishment and sudden abandonment of Machu Picchu, this is one of the most popular treks in the world.'

A closer look

When to go: April to October offers the best weather.

Getting there: fly from the UK to Lima and hop on a domestic flight to Cusco from where there is a rail link to the town of Aguas Calientes, at the start of the trail.

Staying there: Aguas Calientes has a good selection of hotels, while camping is the order of the day on the trail itself.

Maps and guides: *Explore the Inca Trail* by Jacquetta Megarry and Roy Davies (Rucksack Readers) details three Inca Trails to Machu Picchu, with excellent mapping.

More information: www.perutourist.info.

Engelberg (Switzerland)

Think Switzerland and most people think of the Alps. However, these massive mountains with their jagged peaks, deep valleys and snaking glaciers represent only a small proportion of the hiking possibilities in this country.

Head for the village of Engelberg in central Switzerland and you will find a family-friendly destination with trails of all levels of difficulty, from short nature rambles to more challenging upland ascents.

Chairlifts and cable cars offer easy access to higher ground and marked routes include a hike to see marmots, which kids will love, an invigorating lake circuit or more challenging summit ascents.

Engelberg prides itself on its gastronomy, so look forward to a great meal at the end of a day in the mountains.

A closer look

When to go: the summer season runs from June to September.

Getting there: Engelberg is an hour and a half's drive (or bus ride) south of Zurich.

Staying there: no shortage of accommodation, with something for all budgets.

Maps and guides: buy a copy of the 1:25,000 scale Engelberg Hiking Map on arrival.

More information: www.engelberg.ch.

Dolomites via ferrata (Italy)

A must for thrill-seekers, via ferrata is the use of fixed ladders, chains, rungs, wires and bridges to negotiate steep gorges and sheer cliffs where walkers would otherwise fear to tread. The first such route was developed in Austria in the 1840s, but they really came into their own in Italy during the First World War as a means of moving troops and equipment through the Dolomite mountains.

After the war the military abandoned them and over time the routes were adopted by walkers and climbers and their recreational use spread across the Continent. Rare in the UK – there is one at Honister in the Lake District – via ferrata fans must travel to countries like Italy, France, Switzerland and Austria where a growing appetite for this type of adventure is fuelling a new wave of routes with something for everyone, from families with young children to seasoned pros.

Few areas, however, can compete with the Dolomites in terms of the sheer number and variety of via ferrata routes. Unlike climbing, the only specialist equipment you need is a pair of shoes with excellent grip plus a helmet and a harness, which can usually be hired.

For beginners, the best way to start is to book a specialist via ferrata holiday or engage the services of a reputable guide.

> 'A must for thrill-seekers, via ferrata is the use of fixed ladders, chains, rungs, wires and bridges to negotiate steep gorges and sheer cliffs where walkers would otherwise fear to tread.'

A closer look

When to go: July to September.

Getting there: the Dolomites are located in northeast Italy. Venice Marco Polo and Venice Treviso, both of which welcome budget flights from the UK, are the closest airports.

Staying there: choose from small family run hotels, cheap bed and breakfasts or well-equipped apartments.

Maps and guides: *Via Ferratas of the Italian Dolomites: North, Central and East* by John Smith and Graham Fletcher (Cicerone).

More information: www.viaferrata.org.

Summing Up

These are just a few of the many overseas destinations offering great walking country. A hiking holiday is a great way to escape the tourist hotspots and spend time exploring more out of the way places that many visitors will never see. A walking holiday does not have to be all about walking. You can also enjoy traditional local food and drink, learn about different cultures and immerse yourself in a completely different way of life. Go it alone or seek out one of the many tour operators that specialise in walking holidays.

Chapter Ten

One Step Further

Tackling mountains

What is a mountain and how does it differ from a hill? According to the Oxford English Dictionary, a mountain is 'a mass of land rising abruptly and to a large height from the surrounding level'. Other reference works suggest the cut off point between a hill and a mountain is 2,000 feet, or approximately 610 metres.

Mountains present a greater challenge for the walker, not least because they often require lengthy stretches of frequently strenuous ascent and descent. There are other demands too. At altitude, weather can be more hazardous than on low ground. It can be much colder and conditions can change more rapidly. The terrain can be harsher and the underfoot conditions rougher and less forgiving.

However, do not let this put you off. Mountain climbing is an extremely rewarding activity, not least because of the spectacular views the summits afford.

Some mountains to try

If you fancy moving on to mountains, overleaf are some routes for novices planning the big step up.

'Mountains present a greater challenge for the walker, not least because they often require lengthy stretches of frequently strenuous ascent and descent.'

Schiehallion

One of Scotland's most popular mountains, the 'fairy hill of the Caledonians' is a distinctive conical peak offering superb views over the wild lands of Rannoch Moor and Glencoe. Generations of hikers have cut their mountaineering teeth on this one.

A closer look

Where: Southern Highlands, Scotland.

Distance: 6 miles/10km.

Height: 3,554ft/1,083m.

Start/finish: Braes of Foss car park (grid ref NN 752 557).

Map: OS Explorer 386.

Route: thanks to the work of the John Muir Trust, a new path now rises over the eastern flank of Schiehallion from Braes of Foss to the summit, replacing the old path that had become badly eroded. Return by the same route.

Ben Lomond

Within easy reach of Glasgow and set in the heart of the Loch Lomond and the Trossachs National Park, a path leads all the way from Rowardennan, on the banks of Loch Lomond, to the summit.

A closer look

Location: Loch Lomond and the Trossachs National Park, Scotland.

Distance: 7 miles/11km.

Height: 3,194ft/974m.

Start/finish: car park next to pier at Rowardennan (grid ref NS 359 987).

Map: OS Explorer 364.

Route: a path signed for Ben Lomond leaves the car park and climbs through a Forestry Commission plantation. It emerges on to open hillside and swings north, rising steeply to Sron Aonaich. The ascent continues up the southern shoulder of Ben Lomond, the gradient increasing as the summit is approached. Return by the same route.

Arenig Fawr

Located between Bala and Trawsfynydd, the Arenigs are often overlooked by those heading to the more popular mountains of Snowdonia. However, on a clear day the solitary summit of Arenig Fawr offers superb views over every major summit in the national park.

A closer look

Location: South Snowdonia, Wales.

Distance: 7 miles/11.2 km.

Height: 2,802ft/854m.

Start/finish: Arenig quarry (grid ref SH 831 392).

Map: OS Explorer OL18.

Route: walk east along a lane from the car park to join a grassy track just beyond Pant-yr-Hedydd. The route rises to Llyn Arenig Fawr reservoir and continues on a spur south of the lake to the summit. Descend northeast, following a fence for a mile and then drop into the wide cwm (curved depression) on the left to avoid steep crags. A vague path descends across open hillside. Pick up a stream that leads to a grassy track. Once on the track, turn right to return to the start.

Pen y Fan

Pen y Fan is the highest peak in the Brecon Beacons National Park, a rugged range of mountains and hills jostling for position along the border between England and Wales.

A closer look

Location: Brecon Beacons, Wales.

Distance: 5 miles/8km.

Height: 2,907ft/886m.

Start/finish: Pen y Fan car park, near Cwmgwdi (grid ref SO 024 248).

Maps: OS Explorer OL12.

Route: follow the well-defined footpath to Cefn Cwm Llwych. The ridge ascent is initially steep but the gradient eases as height is gained, and there are great views of neighbouring peaks. The final section of the climb to the summit is again steep but straightforward. Return to the car park by the same route.

'It is not the mountain we conquer, but ourselves.'
Sir Edmund Hillary.

Great Gable

Great Gable is one of the best-known peaks in the Lake District and neighbour to the highest mountain in England, Scafell Pike. Fit hillwalkers often bag the pair in one outing, but this route returns home via a delightful mountain tarn (a small lake).

A closer look

Location: Lake District, England.

Distance: 5.5 miles/9km.

Height: 2,949ft/899m.

Start/finish: Seathwaite (grid ref NY 235 121).

Map: OS Explorer OL4.

Route: from Seathwaite Farm, follow a path along the southern edge of the campsite, cross the bridge and prepare for a steep climb alongside waterfalls. At the top, the gradient eases and the path follows Sour Milk Gill up into the mountain pass between Brown Base and Green Gable. Continue to the summit of Green Gable, descend steeply through Windy Gap and make the final ascent of Great Gable over steep and stony ground. Descend southeast on a steep path towards Styhead Tarn, then follow the path running northeast to Stockley Bridge. A track leads north from here to Seathwaite.

Grisedale Pike

For a lesson in mountain walking in the Lake Distrist, there are few better tutors than Grisedale Pike. This shapely peak offers a long, elevated approach over open hillside followed by a moderate descent and a pleasant valley walk home.

A closer look

Location: Lake District, England.

Distance: 6 miles/10km.

Height: 2,594ft/791m.

Start/finish: walkers' car park, a quarter of a mile north of Braithwaite on B5292 (grid ref NY 227 237).

Map: OS Explorer OL4.

Route: a signed path climbs from the car park on to the long slender ridge that leads towards Grisedale Pike. The walking is initially easy but as the peak nears, the gradient becomes increasingly steep over Sleet How until the summit is reached. Descend southwest on a good path to Coledale Hause. Turn left and follow a stony track down to cross Coledale Beck at the stepping-stones below Force Crag mine. A good track leads east, returning you to the start point.

'Climb the mountains and get their good tidings. Nature's peace will flow into you as sunshine flows into trees. The winds will blow their own freshness into you, and the storms their energy, while cares will drop off like autumn leaves.'

John Muir.

Pen-y-ghent

Pen-y-ghent is one of Yorkshire's Three Peaks, a trio of mountains that form a demanding upland circuit for hillwalkers. The route is 25 miles in length and involves over 5,000 feet of ascent. Pen-y-ghent, however, is a fine peak in its own right.

A closer look

Location: Yorkshire Dales, England.

Distance: 8 miles/13km.

Height: 2,276ft/694m.

Start/finish: Horton-in-Ribblesdale railway station (grid ref SD 803 727).

Map: OS Explorer OL2.

Route: follow the Pennine Way from Horton up through Horton Scar to the summit of Pen-y-ghent. Descend south on the Pennine Way for a mile to Churn Milk Hole and turn right heading down Long Lane for two miles to Helwith Bridge. Follow the Ribble Way, alongside the river, back to Horton.

Slieve Binnian

The Mournes are arguably the most spectacular mountains in Northern Ireland, thanks in part to the great granite tors that crown many of the peaks. Slieve Binnian is no exception.

A closer look

Location: County Down, Northern Ireland

Distance: 7 miles/11.2km.

Height: 2,449ft/747m.

Start/finish: car park, Carrick Little (grid ref J 345 219).

Map: OS Northern Ireland sheet 29.

Route: follow a stony track north between fields to a gate and stile. Turn left and follow the Mourne Wall uphill. It leads just about all the way to the top but some easy scrambling is required to negotiate the summit tors. Head north along the crest of the mountain and descend to the col below Buzzard's Roost. Turn right and a good path descends past Blue Lough and Annalong Wood, returning to the gate and stile at the top of the track leading down to Carrick Little.

Peak-bagging

For many people, hillwalking is simply a hobby. However, like most hobbies, there are those who rise to the challenge of collecting or, more accurately, 'ticking off' the various hills and mountains they conquer and it is here that hill tables come into play. These are some of the more popular lists of hills, compiled according to height.

The Munros

The Munros are a roll call of Scottish mountains over 3,000 feet. The original list was drawn up by Sir Hugh Munro and published in 1891. Over the years there have been a number of revisions and the total currently stands at 283. From this has stemmed the popular pursuit of 'Munro-bagging' – attempting to climb all of the Munros. Some take a lifetime to achieve the goal, while others notch up record-breaking rounds.

The Corbetts

Below the Munros are the Corbetts, a list of Scottish peaks over 2,500 feet in height but under 3,000 feet with a re-ascent of 500 feet on all sides, compiled by Mr J. Rooke Corbett. There are currently 219 and, like the Munros, the table is subject to occasional revision.

The Donalds

Donalds are hills in the Scottish Lowlands measuring 2,000 feet in height and above, originally compiled by Mr Percy Donald. There are currently 89 of these.

The Grahams

The Grahams are a complete list of Scottish hills between 2,000 and 2,499 feet high. The table was compiled by Alan Dawson and Fiona Torbet (nee Graham) and contains 224 peaks, including many Donalds.

Long-distance trails

Britain has a network of long-distance paths, signposted routes offering multi-day treks through some of the country's finest scenery. In England and Wales they are known as National Trails, while in Scotland they are called Long Distance Paths.

The majority are linear, running from one place to another and walkers can either set off to complete the whole route or simply enjoy day walks over individual sections. They are a great focus for walking holidays.

Along the way, refreshments and accommodation can be found in towns and villages and, if you don't fancy carrying all your kit with you, local companies or tour operators usually offer a luggage transport service, moving your bags from one overnight halt to the next.

How many long-distance trails are there?

There are 15 National Trails in England and Wales, four official Long Distance Paths in Scotland and one in Northern Ireland. A growing number of unofficial long-distance trails offer equally good outings.

Most trails have accompanying guidebooks, maps and websites, and accommodation options are usually plentiful, so you can opt to stay in comfortable hotels or B&Bs, youth hostels or campsites, depending on your budget.

Public transport is typically good, offering easy access to start points and locations along the way.

How can I find out more?

Details of National Trails in England and Wales can be found at www.nationaltrail.co.uk.

Scotland's Long Distance Paths each have their own website:

- West Highland Way – www.west-highland-way.co.uk.
- Great Glen Way – www.greatglenway.com.
- Speyside Way – www.speysideway.org.uk.
- Southern Upland Way – www.southernuplandway.gov.uk.

Information on the Ulster Way in Northern Ireland can be found at www.walkni.com/ulsterway.

Backpacking

'Backpacking enables fit and experienced walkers to reach the more remote corners of the countryside.'

Backpacking and long-distance walking are very similar activities. However, while a good many long-distance walkers following formal trails take advantage of luggage transfer services to lessen the load on their shoulders, backpackers carry with them everything they need to survive in the great outdoors. Self-reliance is the key for a successful backpacking trip.

Backpacking enables fit and experienced walkers to reach the more remote corners of the countryside and allows hikers to create their own long-distance walks, whether it is a weekend out or a longer expedition.

Backpacking kit

Most backpackers take with them some form of shelter enabling them to camp out in places where there is no accommodation. This can take the form of a lightweight tent or a bivibag (a simple waterproof cover for a sleeping bag).

Backpackers also take with them a sleeping bag and sleeping mat, spare clothing, a towel and wash kit, cooking equipment and enough food to last the length of their expedition (or until they pass through a village or town where they can stock up). The weight soon adds up, but there is plenty of lightweight kit available – and the real art of backpacking is selecting exactly what you need to take with you without weighing yourself down too heavily.

Wild camping

Wild camping is camping on land without formal campsites. Although there are no facilities to hand, the freedom to pitch a tent on your own little spot, miles from anywhere, to enjoy uninterrupted views across open countryside more than compensates. Divest of the shackles of civilisation, there really is no better way to spend a few peaceful nights out.

Where can I camp wild?

Wild camping is acceptable across most of the UK. Provided you stay away from houses and farms, try to be as inconspicuous as possible and behave responsibly, you should encounter no problems.

As with access, the law on wild camping differs between England and Wales and Scotland. In Scotland, there is a long tradition of wild camping and under current legislation anyone can camp wherever access rights apply, as long as it is done responsibly. In England and Wales, there is no legal right to wild camping and permission should be sought before pitching, although this is not always practical. Generally speaking, wild camping is accepted in mountain and hill areas, provided it is above farm intake walls (the walls between pasture and the higher rough ground) and for just a short time – a night or two at most.

Here are a few tips to help you get the most out of wild camping:

- Find a flat, sheltered spot well away from houses and farms, and don't camp on agricultural land.

- Watercourses and lakesides are important sites for birds and animals, so avoid the temptation to camp immediately beside them.

- Short grass is the best terrain to camp on.

- Before you pitch, clear the site of stones, twigs, pinecones and anything else that could lead to an uncomfortable night's sleep.

- Avoid camping on or near boggy, marshy and reedy areas – they are a haven for irritating insects like midges.

- Try to be as inconspicuous as possible and pitch well away from other campers.

- If there are 'no camping' signs, respect them.

- Pack a small trowel to dig a hole for toilet duties.

- Bag up all your rubbish and carry it out with you.

- Leave your campsite as you found it.

Bothies

Bothies are simple, unlocked shelters offering walkers refuge from bad weather.

Where can I find a bothy?

The Mountain Bothies Association (MBA) maintains around 100 bothies. The majority are in Scotland, but there are some in northern England and Wales too. Locations can be found on the MBA's website (www.mountainbothies.org.uk), alongside useful information on bothy use.

Numerous other bothies exist outside the MBA network, most of them hidden away in remote valleys. These are more difficult to find, as their locations tend to be kept secret to prevent overuse or vandalism.

What can I expect to find at a bothy?

Bothies offer no home comforts. Many are former shepherd's cottages or abandoned estate buildings. There may be some rudimentary items of furniture, such as tables, chairs and sleeping platforms. Some have fireplaces or stoves and a few of the more popular ones are equipped with composting toilets. Generally, however, there is no electricity, running water or sanitation.

Will I have the bothy to myself?

As bothies are open to all, it is difficult to predict whether or not you will meet others during your stay. Sometimes you enjoy a peaceful night with the place to yourself, or others may come, tales will be exchanged and drinks swapped by a roaring fire. Bothies can be solitary spots or hubs of social interaction. That is one of the great joys of staying in a bothy – you never know whom you will meet and more often than not passing strangers quickly become firm friends.

'Sometimes you enjoy a peaceful night with the place to yourself, or others may come, tales will be exchanged and drinks swapped by a roaring fire. Bothies can be solitary spots or hubs of social interaction.'

Summing Up

The great outdoors beckons – step up to a new challenge, whether it be tackling a mountain or bagging a whole set of peaks, sampling one of the country's official long-distance trails or packing your kit on your back and making your own way into the wilderness. Whether you choose to camp, stay over in a bothy or walk between towns and villages where a comfortable bed may be found, extend your walks and you quickly extend your horizons.

Help List

Access

Fieldfare Trust

Volunteer House, 69 Crossgate, Cupar, Fife, KY15 5AS
Tel: 01334 657708
www.fieldfare.org.uk
Works with people with disabilities and countryside managers to improve access to the countryside for everyone.

Paths for All

www.pathsforall.org.uk
Promotes the development of multi-use path networks in Scotland.

Scottish Rights of Way and Access Society

24 Annandale Street, Edinburgh, EH7 4AN
Tel: 0131 558 1222
info@scotways.com
www.scotways.com
Protects and develops access to the Scottish countryside.

Accommodation

See also tourist boards.

Hostelling International (Northern Ireland)

www.hini.org.uk
Youth hostel accommodation across Northern Ireland.

Independent Hostel Guide

www.independenthostelguide.com
Independent hostels, bunkhouses and camping barns across the UK and overseas.

Scottish Independent Hostels

www.hostel-scotland.co.uk
Independent hostels north of the border.

Scottish Youth Hostel Association

www.syha.org.uk
Runs a network of 60 youth hostels in Scotland.

Youth Hostel Association

www.yha.org.uk
Operates over 200 hostels in England and Wales.

Canals and waterways

British Waterways

www.waterscape.com
Operates and maintains Britain's canals and waterways and promotes recreational use.

Conservation

John Muir Trust

www.jmt.org
Owns and manages wild land estates in the highlands and islands of Scotland and runs the John Muir Award.

Mountain Bothies Association (MBA)

www.mountainbothies.org.uk
Maintains over 100 open bothies in Scotland, northern England and Wales.

National Trust

www.nationaltrust.org.uk
Britain's biggest landowner. The National Trust protect and open to the public over 350 historic houses, gardens and ancient monuments.

National Trust for Scotland

www.nts.org.uk
Owns and manages a number of key mountain areas in Scotland.

Scottish Wild Land Group

www.swlg.org.uk
Works to protect and conserve wild land throughout Scotland.

Upland Path Trust

www.uplandpathtrust.org
Protects upland paths throughout the UK.

Countryside agencies

Countryside Access and Activities Network

The Stableyard, Barnett's Demesne, Malone Road, Belfast, BT9 5PB
Tel: 028 9030 3930
info@countrysiderecreation.com
www.countrysiderecreation.com
Works to improve and develop access to Northern Ireland's countryside.

Countryside Council for Wales

Maes-y-Ffynnon, Penrhosgarnedd, Bangor, LL57 2DW
Tel: 0845 130 6229
www.ccw.gov.uk

The countryside agency for Wales.

Leave No Trace Ireland

info@leavenotraceireland.org
www.leavenotraceireland.org
Leave No Trace is an outdoor ethics programme rather than a code, designed to promote and inspire responsible outdoor recreation through education, research and partnerships.

Natural England

1 East Parade, Sheffield, S1 2ET
Tel: 0845 600 3078
enquiries@naturalengland.org.uk
www.naturalengland.org.uk
The government's countryside agency for England. Information on the countryside code can also be found on their website.

Scottish Natural Heritage

Great Glen House, Leachkin Road, Inverness, IV3 8NW
Tel: 01463 725000
enquiries@snh.gov.uk
www.snh.org.uk
The Scottish government's countryside agency. You can view the access code at www.outdooraccess-scotland.com.

Forests and woodlands

Forestry Commission

England
620 Bristol Business Park, Coldharbour Lane, Bristol, BS16 1EJ
Tel: 0117 906 6000
fcengland@forestry.gsi.gov.uk
www.forestry.gov.uk
Scotland
231 Corstorphine Road, Edinburgh, EH12 7AT

Tel: 0131 334 0303
fcscotland@forestry.gsi.gov.uk
www.forestry.gov.uk
Wales
Welsh Assembly Government, Rhodfa Padarn, Llanbadarn Fawr, Aberystwyth,
Ceredigion, SY23 3UR
Tel: 0300 068 0300
fcwenquiries@forestry.gsi.gov.uk
www.forestry.gov.uk
The government's forestry agency owns and maintains working plantations
around the UK and also promotes recreational use of its forests.

The Woodland Trust

Autumn Park, Dysart Road, Grantham, Lincolnshire, NG31 6LL
Tel: 01476 581111
enquiries@woodlandtrust.org.uk
www.woodlandtrust.org.uk
The UK's leading woodland conservation charity.

Mapping

Harvey Maps

12-22 Main Street, Doune, Perthshire, FK16 6BJ
Tel: 01786 841202
sales@harveymaps.co.uk
www.harveymaps.co.uk
Specialist map-making company with a range for walkers.

Ordnance Survey

Romsey Road, Southampton, SO16 4GU
Tel: 0845 605 0505
customerservices@ordnancesurvey.co.uk
www.ordnancesurvey.co.uk
Britain's national mapping agency.

National Parks

Association of National Park Authorities

126 Bute Street, Cardiff Bay, Cardiff, CF10 5LE
Tel: 029 2049 9966
info@anpa.gov.uk
www.nationalparks.gov.uk
Umbrella organisation for national parks in Britain.

Campaign for National Parks

6-7 Barnard Mews, London, SW11 1QU
Tel: 020 7924 4077
info@cnp.org.uk
www.cnp.org.uk
Campaigns to protect and promote national parks in England and Wales.

Scottish Council for National Parks

The Barony, 2 Glebe Road, Kilbirnie, Ayrshire, KA25 6HX
Tel: 01505 682447
info@scnp.org.uk
www.scnp.org.uk
Campaigns to protect and promote national parks in Scotland.

Other information

Avon

www.avon.uk.com
Avon's Skin So Soft lotion is good when used as an insect repellent.

Cordee

www.cordee.co.uk
A website selling specialist walking maps and books.

Hillphones

www.hillphones.info
A recorded information line with details of where shooting is taking place. Visit the website for telephone numbers relevant to your area.

Midge Forecast

www.midgeforecast.co.uk
Visit this website for the midge forecast in Scotland.

St. Andrew's Ambulance Association

www.firstaid.org.uk
St. Andrew's Ambulance provides basic first aid courses. Check the website for locations and prices.

St John Ambulance

www.sja.org.uk
St John Ambulance provides basic first aid courses. Check the website for locations and prices.

Ticktwister

www.ticktwister.co.uk
A product that can safely remove ticks from pets and humans.

O'Tom Tick Twister

www.otom.com
A product that can safely remove ticks from pets and humans.

Sports councils

Sport England

3rd Floor, Victoria House, Bloomsbury Square, London, WC1B 4SE
Tel: 08458 508508
info@sportengland.org
www.sportengland.org

The official sports council for England.

Sport Northern Ireland

2a Upper Malone Road, Belfast, BT9 5LA
Tel: 028 90 381222
info@sportni.net
www.sportni.net
The official sports council for Northern Ireland.

SportScotland

62 Templeton Street, Glasgow, G40 1DA
Tel: 0141 534 6500
sportscotland.enquiries@sportscotland.org.uk
www.sportscotland.org.uk
The official sports council for Scotland.

Sports Council for Wales

Sophia Gardens, Cardiff, CF11 9SW
Tel: 0845 045 0904
scw@scw.org.uk
www.sports-council-wales.org.uk
The official sports council for Wales.

Outdoor training centres

Glenmore Lodge

Aviemore, Inverness-shire, PH22 1QU
Tel: 01479 861256
enquiries@glenmorelodge.org.uk
www.glenmorelodge.org.uk
Scotland's national outdoor training centre.

Plas y Brenin

Capel Curig, Conwy, LL24 0ET
Tel: 01690 720214
info@pyb.co.uk
www.pyb.co.uk
Wales' national mountain centre.

Tollymore Mountain Centre

Bryansford, Newcastle, Co. Down, BT33 0PT
Tel: 028 4372 2158
admin@tollymore.com
www.tollymore.com
Northern Ireland's national centre for mountaineering.

Tourist boards

Northern Ireland Tourist Board

www.discovernorthernireland.com
Official Northern Ireland tourism website.

Visit England

www.enjoyengland.com
England's official tourism website.

Visit Scotland

www.visitscotland.com
Scotland's national tourist board website.

Visit Wales

www.visitwales.co.uk
Wales' tourism website.

Travel and transport

Countrygoer

www.countrygoer.org
Promotes car free travel to the countryside.

National Rail Enquiries

Tel: 0845 748 4950
www.nationalrail.co.uk
Online rail timetables and fare information.

Transport Direct

www.transportdirect.info
Free online journey planner for drivers and users of public transport.

Traveline

www.traveline.org.uk
Plan travel by bus, train and ferry across the UK.

Walking organisations

British Mountaineering Council

The Old Church, 177-179 Burton Road, West Didsbury, Manchester, M20 2BB
Tel: 0161 445 6111
office@thebmc.co.uk
www.thebmc.co.uk
The BMC exists to protect the freedoms and promote the interests of climbers, hill walkers and mountaineers.

British Walking Federation

Ground Floor, 5 Windsor Square, Silver Street, Reading, RG1 2TH
info@bwf-ivv.org.uk
www.bwf-ivv.org.uk
Member clubs organise events designed for walkers of all ages and abilities.

Disabled Ramblers

www.disabledramblers.co.uk
Organises a programme of group walks and events and campaigns for improved access for disabled people.

Forth & Tay Disabled Ramblers

www.ftdr.com
Scottish sister organisation of Disabled Ramblers.

Long Distance Walkers Association

membership@ldwa.org.uk
www.ldwa.org.uk
An association for people who enjoy long-distance walking.

Mountain Aid

www.mountainaid.org.uk
Raises funds to help anyone permanently injured on the Scottish hills and provides financial support to Scottish mountain rescue teams.

Mountaineering Council of Scotland

The Old Granary, West Mill Street, Perth, PH1 5QP
Tel: 01738 493942
info@mcofs.org.uk
www.mcofs.org.uk
Representative body for walkers and climbers who live in Scotland or who enjoy Scotland's mountains.

Ramblers Association

2nd Floor Camelford House, 87-90 Albert Embankment, London, SE1 7TW
Tel: 020 7339 8500
ramblers@ramblers.org.uk
www.ramblers.org.uk
Campaigns to protect and improve access to the countryside and operates a
network of local groups that organise walks and events.

Ramblers Scotland

Kingfisher House, Auld Mart Business Park, Milnathort, Kinross, KY13 9DA
Tel: 01577 861222
scotland@ramblers.org.uk
www.ramblers.org.uk/scotland
The Scottish arm of the Ramblers Association.

Ramblers Wales

3 Coopers Yard, Curran Road, Cardiff, CF10 5NB
Tel: 029 2064 4308
cerddwyr@ramblers.org.uk
www.ramblers.org.uk/wales
The Welsh arm of the Ramblers Association.

Royal National Institute for the Blind (RNIB)

Tel: 0303 123 9999
www.rnib.org.uk
Contact the RNIB for information on rambling and hillwalking for visually
impaired people.

Ulster Federation of Rambling Clubs

4 Woodvale Park, Dungannon, BT71 6DB
secretary@ufrc-online.co.uk
www.ufrc-online.co.uk
Governing body for rambling and hillwalking clubs in Northern Ireland.

Walkers Association of Ireland

www.walkersassociation.ie
An umbrella group for Irish hillwalkers.

Walking websites

Car Free Walks

www.carfreewalks.org
Easy-to-use guides to walks that start and finish at train stations or bus stops.

Countryside Code Wales

www.countrysidecodewales.org.uk
Advice for following the countryside code in Wales.

Go4awalk

www.go4awalk.com
Packed with walk ideas and route guides.

Outdoor Access Scotland

www.outdooraccess-scotland.com
Information on the Scottish Outdoor Access Code to be followed while walking
in the countryside.

Walk Highlands

www.walkhighlands.co.uk
Website with over 1,000 Scottish walk routes.

Walk Northern Ireland

www.walkni.com
Online guide to walking in Northern Ireland.

Walking and Hiking

www.walkingandhiking.co.uk
Lots of useful advice and information for walkers.

Walking Britain

www.walkingbritain.co.uk
A massive database of British walks and information.

The Walking Englishman

www.walkingenglishman.com
Offers dozens of free English walk routes.

Walking for Health

www.whi.org.uk
The Natural England website promoting walking as a way of becoming and keeping healthy.

Walking Forum

www.walkingforum.co.uk
Forum discussing all aspects of country walking and hiking in the UK.

Walking Scotland

http://walking.visitscotland.com
Scotland's national tourist board specialist walking website.

Walking Wales

www.walking.visitwales.com
Wales' specialist walking tourism website.

Walks – country and coast

www.walks.cc
Growing database of free walk routes, primarily in Scotland.

Walks with Wheelchairs

www.walkswithwheelchairs.com
Free database of walks for wheelchair users.

Weather forecasts

BBC Weather

www.bbc.co.uk/weather
Online short and long range forecasts.

Met Office

www.metoffice.gov.uk
UK weather forecasts from the nation's official weather agency.

Mountain Weather Information Service

www.mwis.org.uk
Specialist forecasts covering eight mountain areas in Britain.

Sportscotland Avalanche Information Service

www.sais.gov.uk
Snow conditions and avalanche warnings for Scottish mountains.

Young people's organisations

Duke of Edinburgh Award

Gulliver House, Madeira Walk, Windsor, Berkshire, SL4 1EU
Tel: 01753 727400
info@dofe.org
www.dofe.org
The award includes an expedition section where young people can develop a
full range of outdoor skills.

Girlguiding UK

www.girlguiding.org.uk
Organisation for girls and young women aged from five to 25.

The Scout Association

Gilwell Park, Chingford, London, E4 7QW
Tel: 0845 300 1818
info.centre@scout.org.uk
www.scouts.org.uk
Organisation for boys and girls with a strong outdoor ethos.

Book list

Explore the Inca Trail
By Jacquetta Megarry and Roy Davies, Rucksack Readers, Dunblane, 2006.

Knapsacked Travel – The Slovak Paradise
By Daniel Kollar, Dajama, Slovakia, 2001.

Le Guide Rando: Gavarnie-Luz
By Michael Record, Rando Editions, France, 2006.

Scottish Hill Tracks
By Clifford Stone, Scottish Rights of Way and Access Society, Edinburgh, 2004.

Via Ferratas of the Italian Dolomites: North, Central and East
By John Smith and Graham Fletcher, Cicerone, Cumbria, 2009.

Walking in Corsica
By Gillian Price, Cicerone, Cumbria, 2006.

Western Crete Landscapes
By Jonnie Godfrey and Elizabeth Karslake, Sunflower Books, Exeter, 2005.

Need - 2 - Know

Available Titles Include ...

Allergies A Parent's Guide
ISBN 978-1-86144-064-8 £8.99

Autism A Parent's Guide
ISBN 978-1-86144-069-3 £8.99

Drugs A Parent's Guide
ISBN 978-1-86144-043-3 £8.99

Dyslexia and Other Learning Difficulties
A Parent's Guide   ISBN 978-1-86144-042-6 £8.99

Bullying A Parent's Guide
ISBN 978-1-86144-044-0 £8.99

Epilepsy The Essential Guide
ISBN 978-1-86144-063-1 £8.99

Teenage Pregnancy The Essential Guide
ISBN 978-1-86144-046-4 £8.99

Gap Years The Essential Guide
ISBN 978-1-86144-079-2 £8.99

How to Pass Exams A Parent's Guide
ISBN 978-1-86144-047-1 £8.99

Child Obesity A Parent's Guide
ISBN 978-1-86144-049-5 £8.99

Applying to University The Essential Guide
ISBN 978-1-86144-052-5 £8.99

ADHD The Essential Guide
ISBN 978-1-86144-060-0 £8.99

Student Cookbook - Healthy Eating The Essential Guide
ISBN 978-1-86144-061-7 £8.99

Stress The Essential Guide
ISBN 978-1-86144-054-9 £8.99

Adoption and Fostering A Parent's Guide
ISBN 978-1-86144-056-3 £8.99

Special Educational Needs A Parent's Guide
ISBN 978-1-86144-057-0 £8.99

The Pill An Essential Guide
ISBN 978-1-86144-058-7 £8.99

University A Survival Guide
ISBN 978-1-86144-072-3 £8.99

Diabetes The Essential Guide
ISBN 978-1-86144-059-4 £8.99

View the full range at **www.need2knowbooks.co.uk**. To order our titles,
call **01733 898103**, email **sales@n2kbooks.com** or visit the website.

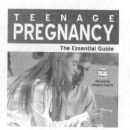

Need - 2 - Know, Remus House, Coltsfoot Drive, Peterborough, PE2 9JX